# Students' Money Matters

A guide to sources of finance
and money management

4TH EDITION

Gwenda Thomas

# TROTMAN

This fourth edition published in 1998
in Great Britain by
Trotman and Company Limited
12 Hill Rise, Richmond, Surrey TW10 6UA

© Gwenda Thomas & Trotman and Company Limited

Foreword © Tony Higgins

*Students' Money Matters* is developed from a major
survey conducted among students throughout the UK
by Trotman and Company Limited.
Developed from an original idea by Andrew Fiennes
Trotman.

*British Library Cataloguing in Publication Data*

A catalogue record for this book is available from the
British Library

ISBN 0 85660 371 6

Typeset by Type Study, Scarborough, North Yorkshire
Printed and bound in Great Britain by
Creative Print & Design (Wales) Ltd

# CONTENTS

# SPONSOR'S INTRODUCTION

## Making the most of being a student

Juggling your finances between having a good time and paying your rent can be a hard task. And as a student you'll inevitably have to make the most of a very tight budget.

To make it easier, this new edition of *Students' Money Matters* gives you valuable information on student finance and expenditure across the UK, with tips on how to manage your money throughout student life. To ensure you get the most out of your time at university or college, the advice given here – much of it from past and present students – will help you develop your money management skills so you can reduce the worry about the financial facts of life.

NatWest has more student branches on or near campus than any other bank, meaning we are close at hand if you need help. We have student advisers in all our student branches across the country, with specialist Student Banking Teams at selected NatWest branches. They work with students all year round, suggesting ways to manage on a tight budget and offering practical solutions to cashflow problems. So whenever you need help to make your money go further, you'll know exactly who to turn to.

To find out more about NatWest's student services call 0800 200 400, Monday to Friday 8am to 8pm, Saturday 9am to 6pm, or pop into a local branch today and speak to a member of staff. (We may monitor and record your phone calls with us in order to maintain and improve our service.)

We at NatWest are committed to all our customers and are pleased to be involved with this important guide. We hope you enjoy the book and find it helpful.

# The Adventure BEGINS

Before you even started school, you were asked 'What are you going to be when you grow up?' Your answers have probably altered somewhat over the years, and that initial ambition to become an astronaut has come down to earth! But one thing that hasn't altered is your ambition to work in an environment that is challenging, rewarding, and where there's no limit to how far you can go. That environment is Ford.

Whether you're aiming to continue studying or are wanting to embark on your career now, Ford can offer you the opportunities that will suit your decision. With a globally successful, dynamic and innovative company behind you that really values its people, this is your chance to really go places.

## Engineering and Systems Sponsorship

For school leavers who plan to read an Engineering degree at one of a number of approved higher education institutions, or a Systems/Information Technology degree. This programme allows students to gain a valuable insight into the world of work.

## Management Accountancy Trainee Scheme

Working full-time at Ford, we will support you to study part-time towards full membership of the Chartered Institute of Management Accountants. With your hard work and dedication, you can really make a name for yourself.

---

For specific details of the entry requirements for each scheme, call us on 01268 401166 or write for an information pack to the Recruitment Department, 15/9000, Ford Motor Company Limited, Dunton Engineering Centre, Laindon, Basildon, Essex SS15 6EE.

Please note that applications must be received by 26th February 1999 for the Engineering Sponsorship Scheme and 30th April 1999 for the Systems Sponsorship and Accountancy Schemes.

# FOREWORD

This is the fourth edition of *Students' Money Matters* – a book that has quickly become *the* source of advice to students on how to manage their finances.

In recent years there has been an increase in the number of students who fail to complete their courses, and research has suggested that the single most important reason for this increase is financial pressure.

There is no doubt that one of the most pressing problems for students today is how to manage on the money available to them, whatever the source – eg grant, loan, bank overdraft or parental subvention.

This year, however, the tension is heightened. Student finance has become almost the most contentious issue in higher education since, from the autumn of 1998, all students entering undergraduate higher education for the first time will be faced with the possibility of paying a contribution towards their tuition fees. To make matters more complicated, the system of student maintenance grants is being phased out so that student financial support will come solely from loans.

Cutting through all the political controversy as to whether to charge students tuition fees is right or not, or whether to place the full financial burden of living costs on a student loan is fair, the fact of the matter is that we are now faced with this circumstance and students will need the best possible advice as to how to plot their way through what is clearly going to be a complicated system. Hence, this book.

*Students' Money Matters* helps guide students through the financial minefield so that they have the right infrastructure to support them through their time at university or college. It is required reading for undergraduates (and their parents) who, if they follow its advice and use their traditional ingenuity, will cope with the challenges of a university or college career.

That UCAS supports this book is no gimmick. You could call it enlightened self-interest. UCAS wants to see students exceed and succeed well in their courses for the benefit of the country as a whole. They will not do that without sound financial advice and support.

*MA Higgins*
*Chief Executive*
*Universities and Colleges Admissions Service*

# INTRODUCTION

'When it comes to money, there is no doubt that for most UK students going on to higher education things are tough, and likely to get tougher.' This was how I introduced Students' Money Matters when first published in 1992. I was right. The student grant was cut over three successive years. Now university fees are being introduced for first degree students and the grant will be done away with altogether. So unless you have parents with a bottomless purse or a private income, something has got to fill the gap in resources.

In this, the fourth edition of *Students' Money Matters*, we set out to investigate all the means and methods by which students can provide themselves with an income while studying for a degree, HND or other higher education qualification.

As before, we are not setting out to argue the rights and wrongs of the financial situation students find themselves in – or, in fact, to tell you what to do. The aim of *Students' Money Matters* is to give helpful information and advice; to point out the pros and cons to be considered when seeking sponsorship, loans, overdrafts, work experience, industrial placements, a year out, work abroad, scholarships, etc, and to tell you how to go about getting them. It is for you to weigh up the evidence and information and make your own decisions – because what's right for you could be totally wrong for somebody else.

However, the book does include comments from employers, university tutors, careers advisers and students. As you might expect, the undergraduates with whom we discussed *Students' Money Matters* were very forthright in their views. These have been included, uncensored. There is nothing more valuable or illuminating than a report from the battlefield!

The book also includes information on how much it is likely to cost you to live as a student in different parts of the country, and advice on how to budget.

To produce *Students' Money Matters* we drew up a list of all the questions we thought you, as a student, would want to ask about financing your studies. We then set about finding the answers. As a result, the book is written largely in the form of a dialogue. The answers given have been kept as short, simple and direct as possible. We've cut through all the red tape and official jargon. Where we felt that you might want to dig deeper into a topic, alternative reference material has been suggested, along with appropriate organisations you can contact.

Occasionally you will find information has been repeated. This is to help the reader. There is nothing more irritating when you are trying to glean information quickly, than having to flick from one section to another.

Money, especially the lack of it, can be a depressing subject. We hope you'll find *Students' Money Matters* an illuminating, helpful and amusing read; and that the information given will make your studying time less worrying and a lot more fun.

In the last edition we asked for your comments, criticism and suggestions for the next edition. These are included here along with updated facts and figures, a new survey of the student scene and a new appraisal of the student situation. But nothing is static, least of all the pecuniary plight of students, so please keep those comments coming. It is only by being vigilant and keeping in touch with 'campus correspondents' that we can pass on the right information to those who follow.

Our thanks in helping prepare this book must go to all those students who proved an invaluable source for so much of the information; the employers, financial and higher education institutions who gave vital assistance in the research of the material.

*Gwenda Thomas*

# 1
# THAT'S THE WAY THE MONEY GOES

## How much is it going to cost you to be a student?

... As much as you have, and probably a lot more. Students have always been hard up, but never more so than now.

In the last year there have been numerous stories in the press about students having to give up their degree courses because they just couldn't make ends meet. With the introduction of fees for first degree university courses, the situation is getting ever more difficult. For some it is critical. But we do have over a million students in full-time higher education in the UK at the moment. How are they managing?

Many factors can affect your financial situation. Some students are luckier – or perhaps more determined – than others in:

● raising additional finance
● managing to work as well as study
● choosing to study in cheaper parts of the country
● living at home
● being excellent managers.

While others ...

● find that money slips through their fingers like water
● are great socialisers and imbibers
● take courses which demand that they buy expensive equipment or books, or need to travel
● have expensive tastes and hanker after all the good things of life

- have a wide range of hobbies and interests
- study in expensive areas such as London.

Obviously you should not pick your course where the living is cheapest, but it is as well to know what costs you are likely to face. This first chapter looks at what it is likely to cost *you* to get a degree, HND or any other higher qualification. But first . . .

## What makes so many of you do it?

This year around 400,000 young people will apply for a higher education course in the UK. What is the great attraction? Why do you forefeit the chance of having money in your pocket to become a near-penniless student and increasingly get into debt?

Here are some of the reasons given by students in a Heist Survey, *Higher Education: The Student Experience:*\*

*'There is no one in our family who hasn't got a degree.'*

*'Neither of my parents have been through higher education and they said you are going – full stop.'*

*'People want graduates and you start one or two steps up the ladder.'*

*'I was a chef. I never had much job satisfaction. I wasn't going to be another Roux Brother.'*

*'I didn't want to get halfway up the management ladder and find people with degrees getting the top jobs. I wanted an exciting job at the top.'*

*'I was too lazy to get a job.'*

*'If you go into a job at 18 you will work for 40 years. I wanted to put off working for as long as possible.'*

*'I didn't know what I wanted to do career-wise and thought I might as well keep learning until I did decide.'*

*'I love studying and writing essays.'*

*'A stepping-stone to reality.'*

*'You get an overall development, you get an academic development and you develop socially. Your whole self changes.'*

*'You are experiencing more things from different angles.'*

\* *Available from Heist, The Grange, Beckett Park Campus, Leeds LS6 3QS.*

*'Having been closeted in a girls' school for years, it is quite educational to be let out among men!'*

If we asked everyone now studying in universities and colleges across Britain, we'd get thousands of different answers. But whatever your reason for studying, it's going to be hard going financially for the next few years. How are you going to manage?

## FEES – WILL I HAVE TO PAY THEM?

Yes – but not the whole fee. If you started at university or college in or before 1997, most of your course fee will be paid by your local authority. However, if you are starting a course at the beginning or after the start of the 1998 academic year (September/October), you will have to pay up to £1000 a year towards the cost of your course.

Students who started their course before that date are in luck – they will not have to pay fees, and nor will gap year students who were actually accepted on a university course during 1996–97 but deferred entry to 1998. Some students may be entitled to help with their fees, which is discussed in the next chapter.

To find an additional £3000–£4000 to go to university will add an extra financial burden on students as many of them vociferously pointed out to us.

*'Fees! Many talented young people will be deprived of a university education, which will be detrimental to the country,'* 3rd year Nursing student, London University

*'Paying fees and grants should be a priority with the government – an educated society is a safer and happier one,'* 2nd year Biochemistry student, Kent

*'Thankfully I am in my final year. If I had to contribute to my tuition fees I wouldn't have been able to go to university, and that goes for a lot of my friends,'* 3rd year English student, Cheltenham: anticipated debt with no fees £6000–£7000 plus £1250 overdraft

*'Eventually attending university will be for the privileged only,'* 2nd year Marketing student, Derby

*'If you want a degree and don't have parents to support you, be prepared to get into lots of debt,'* 4th year Fine Arts student, Derby

# YOUR LIVING EXPENSES

These have to be paid for. You may still be entitled to a maintenance grant, although this is being phased out – again, this is discussed in the next chapter – but wherever your finances come from, it's you who will have to eke them out.


# ACCOMMODATION – THE MAJOR DEMAND ON YOUR FINANCES

Accommodation will probably soak up nearly half of your income. If it's full-board in university accommodation then you are looking at over three quarters of your total income.

Finding the right place to live is important, especially in your first year. It can affect your whole attitude to your college, your course, your study, the town or city where you are staying, making the right friends, and whether you actually do well. If it's half an hour's walk, or a bus ride across town to get to the library, you may think twice about going there. If you're stuck in a bedsit with a grumpy landlord, and no other students around you, the weekends could be very long and lonely.

Most institutions give first-year students first claim on halls of residence. But for some students, living with a hundred or so other people, sharing bathrooms, meal times, TV programmes, problems, passions – even bedrooms – can be an unbearable strain. Others thrive on the camaraderie. Criticising mixed colleges, one student told us: 'Coping with an ex-boyfriend over cornflakes and coffee at 8am is something not to be endured.'


## Getting the right information

College prospectuses will generally give you details about halls of residence, though these may not be altogether bias-free. Student unions may also have a view – ask if there's an alternative prospectus or student union handbook. Above all, check out the accommodation for yourself if you can when you make your first visit.

Look at:

- cost
- whether rooms are shared

- eating arrangements – is it full-board, half-board, kitchen/do-it-yourself?
- facilities provided
- distance from college
- transport availability – and frequency
- shops

## Getting help

The college accommodation office is responsible for placing students in halls of residence, and will send you details once you've accepted a place. The accommodation office will also help you to find rented accommodation.

# ACCOMMODATION IN HALLS OF RESIDENCE

## What will it cost?

If you look at our charts (pages 6–7), you will see that costs vary significantly between different types of accommodation. Be aware that the number of meals (two, sometimes three), the number of days per week (usually five or seven), and the number of weeks in the academic year can vary between institutions. The 'other' category includes any other accommodation than the norm such as ensuite, up-to-the-minute facilities or out-of-town accommodation. Costs also vary between universities, with much higher costs especially in the London colleges. Check out exactly what the costs cover and what facilities are provided.

**Points to note:**

- Figures for Oxford, Cambridge and Durham are an average for all colleges; costs for individual colleges vary considerably.
- When comparing self-catering accommodation in halls of residence with the rented sector, remember that with college accommodation, gas and electricity are probably included. This is unlikely to be the case in the rented sector.

# Estimated Weekly Cost of University-Managed Accommodation

| Institution | 2 meals | No food | Other |
|---|---|---|---|
| Aberdeen | £60–76 | £33–50 | £70–93 |
| Abertay, Dundee | | £35.70–49.07 | |
| Anglia | | £40–59 | |
| Aston | £63.48 | £41.48 | |
| Bath | | £40.50 | £48.60 |
| Birmingham | £66.73–84.90 | £37–50 | |
| Bournemouth | | £47.50–50 | |
| Bradford | £63.30 | £36.90–39.40 | £53 |
| Brighton | £62–70 | £42–57 | £43.50–46.50 |
| Bristol | £56–80 | £28–49 | |
| Bristol, University of the West of England | | £38–46.50 | |
| Brunel | £49.90–57.50 | £37–41 | £50 |
| Buckingham | | £55 | |
| Cambridge | £64–75 | £33–44 | |
| Central England in Birmingham | £55 | £38.55 | £34.48 |
| Central Lancashire | | £45.52 | |
| City University | £83 | £71.73 | |
| Coventry | £64.50 | £45 | |
| Cranfield | £58–80 | £45 | |
| De Montfort | £52.90 | £38.85–45.10 | £34.15 |
| Derby | | £46–56 | £37 |
| Dundee | £63.28 | £47.51–51.94 | £34.09 |
| Durham | £70 | £36–52 | |
| East Anglia | | | |
| East London | | | £55.50 |
| Edinburgh | £74–85 | £45–56 | |
| Essex | £78 | £34–53 | |
| Exeter | | £40 | £60 |
| Glamorgan | £67 | £41–48 | |
| Glasgow | £63 | £40 | |
| Glasgow Caledonian | £59 | £35 | £59 |
| Greenwich | £70 | £60 | £50 |
| Heriot Watt | £64.50 | £40.50 | |
| Hertfordshire | | £50 | |
| Huddersfield | £72 | £36 | £34 |
| Hull | £53.55–70 | £39.40–51 | £29.96 |
| Keele University | | £30–54 | |
| Kent at Canterbury | £54 | £43 | |
| Kingston | | £55 | |
| Lancaster | | £30–54 | |
| Leeds | £59.25–70 | £33.73–49.53 | £49.53–57.70 |
| Leeds Metropolitan | | £39–59 | £35 |
| Leicester | £57.54–76.93 | £36 | £36 |
| Liverpool | £66.75 | £44 | |
| Liverpool John Moores | | £39.50–48 | |
| London | | | |
|   Goldsmiths College | £62 | £45–57 | |
|   Guildhall | £70 | £47–67 | |
|   Heythrop College | £78–85 | £48–55 | |
|   Imperial College | £58.59–76.58 | £24.50–63.07 | |
|   Jews' College | | £50.55 | |
|   King's College | £76.30–109.20 | £37.87–59.92 | £70 |
|   Queen Mary & Westfield | | £57–71 | £59 |
|   Royal Free Hospital | | £50 | |
|   Royal Holloway | £80 | £55 | |
|   Royal Veterinary College | £75–90 | £45–57 | £45 |
|   School of Economics | £91 | | |
|   School of Oriental & African Studies | | £70 | |
|   School of Pharmacy | £85 | £75 | |

| | 2 meals | No food | Other |
|---|---|---|---|
| *London continued* | | | |
| School of Slavonic & E. European Studies | £83 | | £50 |
| St George's | | | £44 |
| St Mary's | £65–85 | £63 | |
| University College | £80 | £41–77 | |
| Wye College | £69 | | |
| Loughborough | £67 | £38 | |
| Luton | | £50–52 | |
| Manchester | £66 | £36.40–83.16 | |
| Manchester Institute of Science & Technology | £60 | £50 | |
| Manchester Metropolitan | £63.30 | £41.50 | £55.10 |
| Middlesex | | £49.55 | |
| Napier | | £50 | |
| Newcastle upon Tyne | £56.85 | £34.46 | |
| North London | £70 | £55 | |
| Northumbria at Newcastle | £65.50 | £40–42.50 | £51.50 |
| Nottingham | £69.60 | £32 | |
| Nottingham Trent | £65.74 | £51.70–53.90 | |
| Oxford | £89.70 | £58.87 | |
| Oxford Brookes | £68 | £46 | |
| Paisley | | £27.97–33.50 | |
| Plymouth | | £30–39.99 | |
| Portsmouth | £56–66 | £36–50 | |
| Queen's, Belfast | £57 | £38.50–43 | |
| Reading | £59–87.70 | £37.80–56.50 | |
| Robert Gordon | | £44–59 | |
| St Andrews | £59.92 | £35 | |
| Salford | £64.40 | £34.65–44.10 | |
| Sheffield | £65.05–83.95 | £34.50–56.60 | |
| Sheffield Hallam | £63.30 | £45.50 | |
| South Bank | | £58–70 | |
| Southampton | £70–74 | £38–42 | |
| Staffordshire | | £27–53 | £55–90 |
| Stirling | | £45 | |
| Strathclyde | £62.05 | £43.35 | £56.60 |
| Sunderland | £56.50–57.50 | £29–43 | |
| Surrey | | £37–53.89 | |
| Sussex | | £45.50 | |
| Teesside | £44.92 | £37.42–45.30 | £29 |
| Ulster | £32.50–£36 | | |
| Wales | | | |
| Aberystwyth | £53 | £27.87 | |
| Bangor | £54–57 | | £38 |
| Cardiff | £56 | £47 | |
| Lampeter | £67 | £39.50 | £38.80 |
| Newport | | £45 | £39 |
| Swansea | £66.40 | £37 | £51.75 |
| Warwick | £63.25 | £34.30–50.65 | |
| Westminster | | £65 | |
| Wolverhampton | | £37.28 | £43.15 |
| York | | £35.28 | |

Source: *University and College Entrance 1999: The Official Guide*

# Will I have to share a room?

Possibly. In some colleges you may have to share a room for one or two terms. If you do have to share, you will probably be sent a questionnaire designed to find out what sort of person you are and the kind of person you could live with. Typical questions: Would you want to share with a smoker or a non-smoker? Are you an early riser? Do you like to go to bed late and get up late? Are you a party person? What kind of music do you like? Is there any kind you can't stand? Honesty is the only way to harmony. Even if you are easy-going about smoking, do you really want to sleep in a smoky atmosphere? And, although your intentions may be very laudable at the moment, how are you going to feel about your room-mate stomping around at eight in the morning when you've been out partying until two?

# How much is rented accommodation going to cost?

Research carried out by *Students' Money Matters* in January 1998 in higher education institutions throughout the UK revealed some interesting facts. The average cost of rents in London among the students we contacted were predictably higher than anywhere else – on average students were paying £48pw. Apart from London, the south and

## Cash crisis note

- Students in the southeast, but studying outside London, are thought to be suffering particularly badly, as they are being asked to pay London-equivalent rents while not qualifying for the larger grants and student loans given to students who study in the capital.
- 69.6% of students said that accommodation off-campus was easy to find. However. . .
- 69.7% thought it was expensive and 35% thought it was difficult to find suitable accommodation close to their university. In London and the southeast many students spent all the value of their full grant on accommodation.
- More and more students, especially in the south of England are applying to the access funds for help with living with varying degrees of success. £1750 was the highest amount anybody we discovered managed to get though sums of £500–£600 were often mentioned. Those needing help must apply early as funds tend to run out by the second term.
- While some areas report high competition for good accommodation, in Hull, where student numbers have fallen, accommodation is plentiful and rents have actually decreased.

southeast of England, rents in Scotland proved to be higher than in the rest of the country at £49 while in England and Wales generally they were £42. Full details of rents in different parts of the country are on pages 14–15.

## University accommodation

A number of students complained about the high and increased cost in university accommodation. A student at Oxford said that the 'dramatic increase' meant that one third of all undergraduates were under severe financial pressure. Another said her lifestyle was only possible because of generous relatives.

**Action**
Check out the length and terms of your contract – is it for 52 weeks? A recent survey of university students found that more and more landlords were asking students to sign 52-week contracts for accommodation. This means they are paying rent during the Christmas, Easter and three-month summer vacation, when they are likely to be at home.

## Possible problems when renting accommodation

*'The landlord said a verbal tenancy agreement would suffice, yet a couple of months after we moved in he presented a 10-page tenancy agreement for us to sign. I took the agreement to the Accommodation Officer at the university who advised us not to sign the agreement and to leave the flat. We took her advice, served our notice (agreed under the verbal agreement) and left. On leaving we were told that we would get our £200 deposit back once the gas and electricity bills were paid. That was a year and a half ago. We are still waiting. Now the Citizens Advice Bureau advise us that we could be liable for six months rent if we took the case to a small claims court. You just can't win.'* 2nd year student, Stirling University

*'Heating and water not working properly – boiler dangerous. A house with all appliances working is a rarity.'* 3rd year Sociology student, Bradford

*'The shower was broken for six months and the landlady simply did not do anything about our problems.'* 3rd year English/Philosophy student, Leeds

## Rob's Story

The police, the fire-brigade, the environmental health department and a television crew were not the visitors I anticipated when I moved into my first house with seven friends.

Things started to go wrong when the weather turned nasty; it was only then we realised that the roof and windows leaked, there was mould everywhere, you could view the garden through holes in the bathroom and it was so cold even the toothpaste froze. The kitchen ceiling came down, twice, and when it snowed outside it snowed inside as well. There were vermin everywhere. Sit on the sofa and you'd hear this constant nibbling.

Just as a side issue, joyriders blew up a stolen car in our garden – enter the fire-brigade. And a break-in resulted in the disappearance of £2000 worth of our possessions.

Things got worse. We called in the gas board who condemned six out of the seven gas fires and the cooker-grill. We called in the environmental health department who condemned everything and called in a TV crew. But a moment of fame on 'Edit Five' didn't achieve much . . .

We stopped paying rent – around £220 a week. After three months we came down one morning to find the landlord's son and his friends and family sitting in our living room. Somebody called the police who arrived in a riot van, but couldn't help since there was no riot and fortunately nobody wanted to throw the first punch.

It was time to negotiate.

I said I would pay £50 and go in two days if they'd sign to say my rent bill was settled – which they did. Somebody else paid a month's rent. The others just left. The landlord didn't take them to court for non-payment of rent, perhaps he too had had enough.

Since then I have had excellent accommodation and very cooperative landlords, but a life a little short on drama.

*'We found ourselves entertaining unwanted visitors – cockroaches from the cafe downstairs.'* 1st year Modern European Studies student, Thames Valley

*'I was stuck in lodgings miles from anywhere. The buses stopped at 7pm so studying at the library or staying on campus after 6.30 meant paying for a taxi home.'* 2nd year Engineering student, Brunel

## Should I take out insurance?

That's something only you can really decide. You may find your parents' insurance covers you for personal possessions – check that with them first. Otherwise . . .

- If you are living in halls of residence you may well find that there is a comprehensive policy covering all students and your bill will include insurance cover. Check this out before considering taking out any personal insurance cover.

  NatWest offers a basic insurance package which starts with an overall sum of £2500. This includes cover for computers and accessories up to a limit of £750. Premiums start at £33.80 for students living in halls of residence and £44 for those in rented or other accommodation. You then have the choice of increasing your contents cover to £3000 or £4000. This includes increased limits for personal computers, up to £1500 and automatic cover for personal belongings taken outside the home. These rates are being revised and likely to go down later in 1998. Endsleigh offers special computer equipment insurance cover. For students in halls of residence it cost £15pa for equipment valued up to £500 rising to £72pa for equipment valued at £2500. For those in rented accommodation costs are higher and depend on the area where you live. For example: cover for equipment worth £500 would cost £16pa in a 'good' area but £45pa in a crime 'hot spot'. There are some areas in Birmingham, Leeds, Manchester, Sunderland, Teesside and Wolverhampton considered so 'bad', Endsleigh will give no cover at all.

- If you are living in rented accommodation, the landlord of the house or flat you rent should have the premises covered by insurance for -re and structural damage, but it is unlikely to cover your personal possessions. Students tend to keep open house, and because people are coming and going all the time, security is often lax. If you do have a lot of expensive possessions, it might be worthwhile considering insurance, especially if you carry expensive belongings about. Ask yourself: What would it cost me to replace my stereo, TV, video, camera, gold watch, PC, course books, whatever? Compare that with an outlay of say £35–£66 a year. Rates for personal insurance depend on where you live. It costs more if you live in a big city than a sleepy rural town. And in a crime hot-spot rates can be prohibitive.

*'Insurance is so ridiculously high here – £100pa for £1000 cover – it's just not worth having and you can't get cover for a bicycle for love nor money. That's what comes of living in grotty area. As far as insurance is concerned we're right off the map. There are better districts of Liverpool to live in but then the rent goes rocketing up so you can't win. The answer is a stout lock on your room door, and have nothing worth pinching.'* Student, Liverpool University

*'Everybody round here hires a TV so if it walks it's covered by the TV rental company. The same goes for washing machines and all other appliances.'*
Student, Liverpool University

*'We had a microwave and sofa cushions stolen! But mainly it's computers, TVs, stereos.'* 3rd year Genetics student, Birmingham

## Do I have to pay Council Tax?

Students are largely exempt from paying Council Tax. Certainly, if you live in a hall of residence, college, student house or somewhere in which all the residents are students, you will be exempt. If you live in a house where there are already two adults, your presence does not add to the bill. If you live in a house with one adult, that person will not lose their 25% single occupancy discount providing they can give proof of you being a student.

## OTHER LIVING EXPENSES

While your accommodation will probably soak up at least half of your available resources, how are you going to spend the rest?

## Food

Once you have a roof over your head, the next major expense is food, and here our survey showed that costs were fairly similar throughout the country with an average of £28.94 a week. The biggest food bills were found in London. This was not so much from eating at home but the cost of snacks during the day. The two hungriest students we found had weekly food bills of £80 and £90, and were both studying at the University of Buckingham.

*'If you can afford to spend time shopping around, going to the cheap shops and cooking your own food, you can live quite cheaply. If you are pushed for time and nip into the nearest store it can be quite expensive.'* Maths student, Edinburgh

> ## Fast facts for beer drinkers
> Uni bar prices range from £1.00 to £1.65, but imbibers head for Portsmouth or Lancaster where the cheapest pint is 80p

## Socialising/entertainment

Our survey didn't assess how good a 'good time' the students were having, or how often they went out, but for cheapness students in the Midlands seemed to be managing best with a weekly bill averaging about £20. Then came East Anglia with an average of £24. Elsewhere, costs were £25–£31.

## Books

All students said they spent more on books in the autumn term and in their first year than at any other time. Some reported that they'd then taken to using libraries instead of buying, as books were so expensive. It is difficult to give an average figure for books, as what you need to buy depends on your course and how well your college library is stocked in your subject. But taking our own survey as a very general guide, the average figure was £117 per year.

### Points to check
Your university or college may have a second-hand bookshop. Find out before you start purchasing; books are very expensive. Check out your college library. Is it well stocked in books on your subject? Is it close to where you study and where you live?

## Course equipment

In subjects such as architecture, the creative arts and some science based subjects, this can be a major item. Figures of £40–£100 per year were often mentioned and £250–£400 for design materials. Computers are an increasing cost for many students and £1000 plus was often mentioned. The highest figure quoted was £3000.

## Photocopying and stationery

Many students mentioned the high cost of photocopying. For those on courses where study covered topics in a wide range of books rather than

# How students budget around the country

(Rent – figure given is what students questioned said they were actually paying. Figure in brackets is what they estimated the average price for the area to be. Travel costs are using public transport only and do not include private cars etc.)

**Northern Ireland***
*per week*

| | |
|---|---|
| Av. rent | £24.75 |
| Av. food | £14.75 |
| Av. soc./ent. | £30.50 |
| Av. clothes | £ 8.90 |
| Av. laundry | £ 0.63 |
| Av. toiletries | £ 4.25 |
| Av. fuel | not available |
| Av. telephone | not available |
| Av. travel | £10.00 |
| **Total** | **£93.78** |

*per year*

| | |
|---|---|
| Av. books | £148.50 |
| Av. photocopying | not available |
| Av. travel home | not available |

**London**
*per week*

| | |
|---|---|
| Av. rent | £ 67.25 (£67.93) |
| Av. food | £ 35.05 |
| Av. soc./ent. | £ 31.28 |
| Av. clothes | £ 7.16 |
| Av. laundry | £ 3.27 |
| Av. toiletries | £ 4.86 |
| Av. fuel | £ 6.38 |
| Av. telephone | £ 6.04 |
| Av. travel | £ 22.23 |
| **Total** | **£183.52** |

*per year*

| | |
|---|---|
| Av. books | £162.48 |
| Av. photocopying | £ 44.00 |
| Av. travel home | £ 71.92 |

**South**
*per week*

| | |
|---|---|
| Av. rent | £ 51.65 (£48.38) |
| Av. food | £ 30.86 |
| Av. soc./ent. | £ 26.22 |
| Av. clothes | £ 5.45 |
| Av. laundry | £ 3.60 |
| Av. toiletries | £ 4.97 |
| Av. fuel | £ 9.47 |
| Av. telephone | £ 4.88 |
| Av. travel | £ 9.92 |
| **Total** | **£147.02** |

*per year*

| | |
|---|---|
| Av. books | £137.73 |
| Av. photocopying | £ 37.64 |
| Av. travel home | £108.30 |

**North**
*per week*

| | |
|---|---|
| Av. rent | £ 36.43 (£35.06) |
| Av. food | £ 26.06 |
| Av. soc./ent. | £ 30.23 |
| Av. clothes | £ 4.51 |
| Av. laundry | £ 2.19 |
| Av. toiletries | £ 2.94 |
| Av. fuel | £ 9.84 |
| Av. telephone | £ 7.28 |
| Av. travel | £ 4.60 |
| **Total** | **£124.08** |

*per year*

| | |
|---|---|
| Av. books | £100.68 |
| Av. photocopying | £ 21.80 |
| Av. travel home | £ 74.89 |

* Figures for Northern Ireland are taken from the 1998 Student Income and Expenditure Survey (NUS/USI). Average rent and food appears comparatively low because over half NI students live at home and the NUS/USI survey includes them; all other statistics are from *Students' Money Matters* research, which focuses on those living in halls/rented accommodation. Fuel & telephone costs were not available.

## Wales
*per week*

| | | |
|---|---|---|
| Av. rent | £ 42.00 | (£40.83) |
| Av. food | £ 29.83 | |
| Av. soc./ent. | £ 25.00 | |
| Av. clothes | £  3.07 | |
| Av. laundry | £  2.76 | |
| Av. toiletries | £  2.25 | |
| Av. fuel | £  9.33 | |
| Av. telephone | £  6.00 | |
| Av. travel | £  4.25 | |
| Total | £101.90 | |

*per year*

| | |
|---|---|
| Av. books | £133.33 |
| Av. photocopying | £ 36.66 |
| Av. travel home | £ 56.25 |

## Home Counties
*per week*

| | | |
|---|---|---|
| Av. rent | £ 50.74 | (£49.65) |
| Av. food | £ 30.76 | |
| Av. soc./ent. | £ 25.37 | |
| Av. clothes | £  4.43 | |
| Av. laundry | £  3.68 | |
| Av. toiletries | £  3.34 | |
| Av. fuel | £  4.84 | |
| Av. telephone | £  8.77 | |
| Av. travel | £  6.46 | |
| Total | £138.40 | |

*per year*

| | |
|---|---|
| Av. books | £130.66 |
| Av. photocopying | £ 35.55 |
| Av. travel home | £ 70.81 |

## East Anglia
*per week*

| | | |
|---|---|---|
| Av. rent | £ 39.26 | (£40.28) |
| Av. food | £ 26.05 | |
| Av. soc./ent. | £ 24.39 | |
| Av. clothes | £  4.18 | |
| Av. laundry | £  2.98 | |
| Av. toiletries | £  3.65 | |
| Av. fuel | £  5.05 | |
| Av. telephone | £  3.50 | |
| Av. travel | £  4.35 | |
| Total | £113.41 | |

*per year*

| | |
|---|---|
| Av. books | £112.69 |
| Av. photocopying | £ 21.62 |
| Av. travel home | £154.20 |

## Scotland
*per week*

| | | |
|---|---|---|
| Av. rent | £ 49.81 | (£44.32) |
| Av. food | £ 28.65 | |
| Av. soc./ent. | £ 26.21 | |
| Av. clothes | £  4.50 | |
| Av. laundry | £  2.97 | |
| Av. toiletries | £  3.60 | |
| Av. fuel | £  7.58 | |
| Av. telephone | £  4.58 | |
| Av. travel | £  5.83 | |
| Total | £133.73 | |

*per year*

| | |
|---|---|
| Av. books | £111.50 |
| Av. photocopying | £24.58 |
| Av. travel home | £103.41 |

## Midlands
*per week*

| | | |
|---|---|---|
| Av. rent | £ 46.02 | (£43.77) |
| Av. food | £ 26.64 | |
| Av. soc./ent. | £ 20.07 | |
| Av. clothes | £  5.74 | |
| Av. laundry | £  3.24 | |
| Av. toiletries | £  4.77 | |
| Av. fuel | £  6.25 | |
| Av. telephone | £  4.55 | |
| Av. travel | £  6.23 | |
| Total | £123.51 | |

*per year*

| | |
|---|---|
| Av. books | £ 86.15 |
| Av. photocopying | £ 26.55 |
| Av. travel home | £ 78.66 |

## West of England
*per week*

| | | |
|---|---|---|
| Av. rent | £ 48.10 | (£47.00) |
| Av. food | £ 26.11 | |
| Av. soc./ent. | £ 25.80 | |
| Av. clothes | £  3.77 | |
| Av. laundry | £  2.30 | |
| Av. toiletries | £  2.28 | |
| Av. fuel | £  3.25 | |
| Av. telephone | £  5.68 | |
| Av. travel | £  2.27 | |
| Total | £119.56 | |

*per year*

| | |
|---|---|
| Av. books | £ 81.87 |
| Av. photocopying | £ 15.12 |
| Av. travel home | £ 86.91 |

majoring on a few textbooks the cost could be considerable. On average £29 per year was spent on photocopying, however, £100 was a figure frequently mentioned. Stationery was another item which was cited as a significant cost.

## Field trips

Geography, biology and zoology students said that field trips could cost anything from £20–£900 a time and though they are generally annual rather than termly occurrences, they are a compulsory component of many courses.

## Mobile phones

Recent figures how that one in six students have mobile phones. Our research suggests that the approximate annual cost for students is £365. What we couldn't gauge is how much it is costing their friends to phone them on their mobiles.

## Clothing

Average cost: £4.75 per week. As we asked for weekly figures in our survey, the low figure for clothing and the frequency of Nil suggested that it was not a weekly expenditure, more an occasional splash-out. Birthday or Christmas presents and charity shops were often given as an alternative answer. Wry comments such as 'I can't afford it' following a confession that up to £55 a week went on socialising and entertainment suggest that for some students clothes are simply a low priority rather than an unaffordable luxury.

## So – where is the cheapest place to study?

Our research this year puts Wales top of the league for money management. Not surprisingly London is by far the most expensive place to study. The hardest hit students are those studying just that bit too far outside London to qualify for the higher grant, yet still paying the London prices.

## Thrift tips

'*Get an overdraft NOT a credit card. With student overdrafts you don't pay interest,*' 4th year Psychology student, Surrey

'*Give up smoking,*' 1st year Drama student, Bristol

'*Always go to the Freshers' fairs and pick up the free handouts.*' 3rd year Ancient History student, London

'*Buy clothes in charity shops,*' 1st year Medicine student, London

'*If your milk disappears from your fridge, add a little food colouring to make it look less appealing to others.*' 1st year Accountancy student, East Anglia.

## TRAVEL DURING TERM TIME

To survive, it seems you need to be fit. Students said that walking was the major form of getting about – cycling seems to be less popular than it was two years' ago. For many, however, travel was a significant cost, with students in London experiencing the most severe problems in terms of expense and time taken to get to lectures. The average London student spent anything from £5 to £60 a week on travel. Compare this with University of Wales students in Cardiff who tend to walk everywhere. Students studying Medicine based in London can be the hardest hit, as training can often mean attachments to other hospitals with locations as much as 40 miles away (check with your LEA to see if you are entitled to financial help). Scottish students on a grant can claim extra for travel of over approximately £70 a year. On average students in the UK pay £7.30 a week for travel on public transport.

Almost a quarter of students are thought to own a car. This figure includes many mature students who tend to drive longer distances during term time. Figures of £5–£25 were given as the cost of petrol per week.

### Travel check

- **The frequency of local bus services:** A huge number of students complained of the infrequency and unreliability of bus services.

  '*There was a bus, but if it turned up, it was always so full of students I couldn't get on. In the end my dad had to buy me a car.*' Law Student, University of the West of England

*'It's a pain having to get four buses a day in winter especially when it's dark and they don't come.'* Shani, 2nd year English student, Birmingham

- **The last bus:** A number of students complained that in many cities bus services finish early, with no regular service after 10.30pm – a major problem for sociable students in outlying districts. Check on this when choosing accommodation.

  *'The last bus was at 7pm. Hopeless for even the most modest socialising.'* Law student, Bristol

- **The cost of taxis:** If there are a few of you, it might not be prohibitive.
- **What the area is like at night:** A number of students mentioned fear at having to cross parkland from halls of residence with poor lighting and the risk of mugging and 'whatever'. Students in east London complained of badly lit streets where even as early as 5pm they really didn't want to walk. Leeds students said women walking on their own in daylight and at night were often attacked in the Hyde Park/Headingly/Woodhouse area. Edinburgh students said those living in Marchmount have to walk through the 'Meadows' park and there had been some attacks at night. And a Bradford student highlighted the 'threat of attack and Asian versus Student animosity.'

## Other student complaints

- Exeter students said that short cuts to popular student lodgings were badly lit. Manchester students complained of split campuses with a five mile journey between the two. Some Liverpool students said it just wasn't safe to go anywhere on your own at night.
- Many students complained that cycling was a danger, and muggings for mountain bikes was a gripe from Manchester. Students elsewhere complained that theft of bicycles was a problem. They also cited pollution and traffic congestion.

*'I have been knocked off my bike at least twice in the last 18 months.'* John, 2nd year English/Management student, Aberdeen

## How far do most students have to travel to study each day?

A recent survey showed that while most university and college students managed to live either in or relatively close to their place of study, students at the 'new' universities were not so fortunate.

## How much will it cost to get to your college from home?

If you live in Exeter and decide to study in Glasgow, getting there is going to be a major expense and you won't be popping home very often. But if home is Birmingham and you study somewhere close at hand, like Manchester, it's relatively cheap. Coaches are always cheaper than trains, but they take longer and the amount of luggage you can take with you is usually limited.

## STUDENT RAIL AND COACH CARDS

Both the train and coach services offer student reductions, provided you buy their special student cards. These last for a year. One longish journey will more than cover the initial outlay, which is:

Railcard: £18 (February 1998)
Reduction: one-third off all rail fares.
Travel restrictions: currently – if travelling before 10am the minimum cost of the fare is £6 single, £12 return. Check with station for full details.
Coachcard: £8 (February 1998)
Reduction: one-third off all fares.
Travel restrictions: some journeys cost slightly more at certain times such as Friday.

### Travel advice note

- **Restrictions** on cards can change, so always check what is being offered and when you can travel.

- **Look for special reductions**: occasionally the rail or coach companies will have special promotions such as half-price student cards, or half-price fares. They may also give discounts on things like CDs or subscriptions to magazines.

- **Taxi fares:** you may find that your accommodation is some distance from the railway or coach station. If you have a mountain of luggage, hi-fi, guitar, duvet, books etc, you will need to take a taxi – another added expense.

Here are some comparative travel costs from London, based on return fare prices in February 1998. Prices quoted include Young Person's Railcard or Coachcard discount:

## CAN I AFFORD TO RUN A CAR?

If your only income is the standard funding for students most rational people would say no. But since so many students do seem to have cars they must be managing it somehow. A recent survey by Reaction UK claimed nearly half of all students own or use a car. Travel from your home to your university will probably be cheaper by car, but you may also find yourself coming home many more times in a term, acting as chauffeur to the party, and taking trips at weekends. And don't under-estimate the maintenance bills: they can be astronomical, especially on an old car. Then there's the road tax, currently £150pa (which can be purchased half yearly at £82.50), your MOT, and AA/RAC membership which makes sense if you have a tendency to break down. But your biggest outlay will undoubtedly be the insurance.

| London to | Train | Coach |
|---|---|---|
| Edinburgh | +*£43.55 | £23.50 |
| Newcastle | +*£41.60 | £20.00 |
| Manchester | +*£26.05 | £15.75 |
| Nottingham | +*£22.45 | £14.50 |
| Birmingham | £22.10 | £11.00 |
| Cardiff | *£22.45 | £16.00 |
| Bristol | *£18.50 | £13.00 |

*Can't travel on a Friday
+Another £3–£6 can be knocked off price if you book a day in advance, more if you book earlier.

# How much to insure my wheels?

Two wheels or four, it's not going to be cheap or easy.

## 4 wheels

Students lucky enough to have a car may find they don't have much luck finding insurance, especially if they are first time drivers and under 21. Try Endsleigh Insurance. Last year the NUS, worried that many students who ran cars couldn't afford the cost of insurance cover, asked Endsleigh (an insurance company which they part own), to try and find a way to reduce motor insurance premiums for students – which they did, by up to 30%. Now, '*Endsleigh effectively represents the whole student marketplace – some 1.5 million students,*' says Sean Regan, Endsleigh's Communications Officer.

**Word of caution:** think twice about 'fronting', that's the old trick of mum taking out the insurance and naming the student as second driver. If there's a claim and it's discovered that the student is really the main driver, you could find the insurance company won't pay up.

Insurance costs vary, depending not just on who you are, but on where you live. Big city drivers pay a higher premium than, say, country folk. In London the costs are prohibitive. Check out if it is cheaper to take out your insurance from your home address or your university lodgings as Vicky did to her advantage. '*My parents live in London. I am studying in Durham. By taking out my insurance up here I saved well over £50.*'

## Two wheels

Now you might think a bicycle was much easier to insure. But any student intending to take a bicycle to a university, must think in terms of having it pinched, or at least borrowed without permission. Insurance companies certainly do.

## Insurance advice

A good padlock and detachable wheel or saddle should be your first form of insurance. Consider exchanging that expensive mountain bike for something that looks as if it's come off the tip.

## Who to try

**Endsleigh.** In March 1998, for cover on a bicycle worth £150, they were charging £31 in a good area rising to £59 in the most dodgy. There are parts of Birmingham, Liverpool, Leeds, Teesside and Manchester where you could get no cover at all. But remember you've got to take out personal cover as well.

**Typical example:** A 20-year-old male student living in Newcastle NE6, with a full licence for two years, driving a 1989 Renault 5, would expect to pay:

| | |
|---|---|
| Endsleigh | £418.96 |
| Direct Line (Privilege) | £464.33 |
| Norwich Union | £481.70 |
| (figures from Endsleigh) | |

Try also the banks – some offer a fairly good deal.

VERDICT: expensive but well worth considering if your bicycle is your only means of transport.

## How much of a problem is finance to students?

If you talk to students, you soon realise that money is not just a problem but *the* major problem. Even students who were not yet in debt, and so seemed to be managing fairly well, felt that it was their major worry.

## WHAT THE STUDENTS HAD TO SAY

*'I was very fortunate to get into halls – a real blessing. There is always someone's door to knock on.'*

*'The social life is centred on drinking. If you don't drink, making friends can be more difficult.'*

*'When I got my cheque, I went totally mad. Going to the disco – not on books!'*

*'Finances are the big problem. Students go out and spend madly in the first few weeks. Then they realise that it's gone. They go to the bank and ask for more. Most don't know where it's gone.'*

*'Be honest when filling in the accommodation form. You might end up sharing with someone with whom you have nothing in common.'*

# TYPICAL STUDENT BUDGETS

Three students from around the country show how their money goes.

**Andrea, 21, second year Fine Art student at Norwich School of Art and Design on a three-year course**
*Accommodation*: living out in shared house with three other students. Own bedroom, shared lounge, dining room and kitchen plus two bathrooms. *Comment*: it's a large old house, just ten minutes walk from college, but impossible to heat.

| Outgoings | Per month | Per year | Comment |
|-----------|-----------|----------|---------|
| Rent | £160.00 | £1660.00 | That's about average for the area. 12-month contract. Rent reduced to half during the two summer months if not there. |
| Gas | £15.38 | £153.80 | Used for heating and cooking. Undetected gas leak in my bedroom (where I smoke) may have pushed this up – it certainly made me ill. Fortunately NHS is free. |
| Electricity | £7.25 | £72.50 | Lighting, fridge, washing machine, dryer which costs a fortune, TV, stereos etc. |
| Water | £6.75 | £80.50 | |
| Telephone | £26.33 | £263.00 | |
| Food | £80.00 | £720.00 | Bought daily on the way back from college – not an economical means of catering. Fruit and veg mostly. Fish if reduced at Tesco. Can't do the student thing of beans on toast every night. |
| Food out | £32.00 | £320.00 | Sarnies, chocolate, coffee. Hot meals in college just £1.50. Pasta dishes, chips, beans, good fill up – patronised mostly by the lads. |
| Cigarettes | £48.00 | £576.00 | It's my only vice. |
| Magazines | £10.00 | £120.00 | Glossies – needed for my degree. |
| Cosmetics/Toiletries | £16.00 | £192.00 | Excluding make-up generally given as presents. |
| Travel term time | £0 | £0 | Walk everywhere. |
| Travel London | £18.00 | £216.00 | Visiting friends/galleries. |
| Travel home | | £45.00 | Three visits to Lincolnshire during tern – £15 return. Mum drives me – beginning and end of term. |
| Travel Card | £0 | £18.00 | |
| Socialising | £60.00 | £600.00 | Pints in SU or pub when in funds, telly at home when skint. |
| Entertainment | £20.00 | £200.00 | Clubs, cinema etc. |
| Clothes | £18.00 | £216.00 | One splurge a term £40 – no more. Otherwise haunt charity shops. |
| TV licence | | £218.00 | |
| CDs | | £60.00 | One full price and one in sale a term. |
| Laundry | £2.00 | £18.00 | Soap powder. |
| Exhibitions/galleries | £2.00 | £18.00 | Fortunately most galleries are free. |
| Books | | £30.00 | |
| Photocopying | | £15.00 | |
| Art materials | | £350.00 | It's a nightmare. |
| Course levy | | £50.00 | Paid into college so they can buy materials cheaper. |
| Holidays | £0 | £0 | I should be so lucky! |
| Course trips | | £230.00 | Barcelona £100 trip + £100 spending money. College trips to London galleries. |
| Gifts | £0 | £0 | Occasionally charity shops |
| Lottery | £4.00 | £48.00 | |
| Total | | 6293.68 | |

| Income | Per term | Per year | Comment |
|---|---|---|---|
| Grant | £550.00 | £1650.00 | |
| Student Loan | | £1685.00 | Big mistake – took it all out at once. |
| Parental contribution | | £450.00 | Not on regular basis, only when in dire straits. |
| Access | | £30.00 | Help with art materials. |
| Earnings term time | £259.20 | £777.60 | Cleaning fridges M&S food hall keeps me fit – you should see my muscles. |
| Holiday job | | £0 | Worked in the US looking after five children. Earned £500 and spent it. |
| Overdraft | | £1000.00 | Will drop when I get my next grant. Can go up to £1500 in third year without charges. |
| Total | | £5592.60 | |

*Additional comment*: you cannot expect a student to live on cheap toxin-packed foods. It's not good for our performance or mental state. We tried to organise a kitty and eat together but it didn't work. It's such a struggle now and next year I will have to find another £500–£600 for my final degree show. I just don't want to think about where it will come from. Perhaps I'll win the lottery. You can't sacrifice your work for money.

**Robin, 20, second year Maths student at King's College, London University**
*Accommodation*: living out in shared house with one other student. Own bedroom, shared living room, kitchen and bathroom. *Comment*: West Kensington is a nice area and the half-hour tube ride from college isn't far for London.

| Outgoings | Per month | Per year | Comment |
|---|---|---|---|
| Rent | £240.00 | £2880.00 | 12-month contract with water rates included. |
| Electricity | £20.00 | £180.00 | Fridge, lighting, washing machine – over 9 months. |
| Gas | £20.00 | £180.00 | Heating and cooking. |
| Telephone | £40..00 | £360.00 | Unfortunately my girlfriend only has a mobile. |
| Food in | £60.00 | £540.00 | I go home at the weekends which cuts my bills. No kitty but a system of your turn to buy . . . whatever, which surprisingly works. |
| Food out | £20.00 | £180.00 | I work in the uni shop, when dates are up on food, like pasties and sausage rolls, I get them free – a saving of £5–£10 a week. Meal in uni canteen £2–3 – mostly used by lecturers. |
| Toiletries | £16.00 | £192.00 | It's amazing how deodorants disappear. |
| Clothes | £0 | £200.00 | Big spend once I've been paid in the summer, otherwise I rely on presents. |
| Travel term time | £60.00 | £540.00 | Monthly season gives unlimited underground travel on zones 1&2. |
| Travel home | £15.20 | £136.80 | Go home every weekend £3.80 return. |
| Socialising | £120.00 | £1440.00 | Includes meals out. Night clubs are expensive in London. I go out perhaps four nights a week and drink a couple of lagers. |
| Entertainment/sport | £45.00 | £540.00 | Canoeing and sailing. Monthly weekend club trips to Wales or Devon. |
| Cigarettes | £100.00 | £1200.00 | If I think about the cost it makes me nervous so I smoke more. |
| Chocolate | £30.00 | £360.00 | Flatmate and I are unashamedly chocoholics. |
| TV licence | | £43.75 | |
| CDs | | £0 | Flatmate works in Woolworths and gets them cheap. |
| Laundry | £4.80 | £43.20 | Washing machine provided but not washing powder. |
| Books | | £30.00 | Uni has an excellent library. |
| Photocopying | | £30.00 | |
| Holidays | | £120.00 | Canoeing week in Scotland. |
| Flowers | £12.00 | £144.00 | Weekly red rose for girlfriend. |
| Presents | | £450.00 | |
| Course fees | | £550.00 | Repeating year because failed final year exams. Getting the right balance between study, working to survive, social life and interests isn't easy. |
| Interest on credit card | | £43.00 | Currently owe £350 at 12% . I keep paying it off but it sneaks back. |
| Total | | 10,352.75 | |

| Income | Per term | Per year | Comment |
|---|---|---|---|
| Grant | £0 | £0 | I got £1200 last year but as I'm repeating a year, nil. |
| Parental contribution | | £2700 | My parents are giving me extra this year to make up for not getting the grant but I will have to pay it back once I graduate. |
| Student loan | | £2085 | Taken in one payment – big mistake. |
| Access | | £700 | To pay off credit card debts. |
| Earnings term time | £966 | £2760 | Approx 20 hours a week in the student union shop and as a security guard in student union bar. Christmas and Easter hols hours reduced to 10 hours. |
| Earnings holidays | | £2100 | Teaching outdoor pursuits – sailing, canoeing, dragon boating etc. £150 for a 40-hour week for 14 weeks. |
| Overdraft | | £1000 | |
| Student Barclay Card | | £350 | |
| Total | | £11,695 | |

*Comment*: I do a voluntary stint in the student union advice centre so I know just how difficult students find it to manage. They come with all kinds of problems – housing, landlords, academic studies – but it's mostly finance. Sometimes the only possible solution is to take a year out, take a job and get your finances straightened out. I expect to be £6000–£7000 in debt when I leave university that includes overdraft, debt to parents and student loan. You have to be strict with yourself. I withdraw just £50 a week for socialising and when it's gone I don't take out any more.

**Clare, 26, third year Psychology student at Hull University. Clare left school and worked for seven years until suddenly deciding 'my brain was dead'.**
*Accommodation*: Rented flat, shared with two other students with own bedroom, communal living room, kitchen, bathroom and separate toilet (an essential), two miles from the university.

| Outgoings | Per month | Per year | Comment |
|---|---|---|---|
| Rent | £152 | £1824 | That's the higher end for Hull. |
| Electricity/gas/water | £32 | £384 | We put all the bills together and divide them between the three of us. |
| Telephone | £15 | £180 | |
| Food | £80 | £960 | Hull is excellent for cheap food shops and wacking great take away hot pizzas – £2.50 each. |
| Food out | £20 | £240 | Endless coffees, lunch in college £1.80–£2.50. |
| Kitty contribution | £10 | £120 | Coffee, toilet rolls, bread, washing up liquid etc. |
| Toiletries cosmetics | £16 | £192 | Bog standard – fortunately I can resist marketing hype. |
| Laundry | £16 | £152 | |
| Travel term time | £16 | £152 | Bus to college. Occasionally bicycle. |
| Travel home | | £147 | Three visits to Huntington, Cambridge a year – return fair £49. |
| Student rail card | | £18 | |
| Bicycle | £5 | £60 | Family hand-down. I'm buying inner-tubes as if they were going out of fashion. Hull streets are paved with broken glass. |
| Socialising | £20 | £240 | Low for Hull – I did the clubbing and pubbing when younger. Usually friends come round for a meal and wine. |
| Cigarettes | £80 | £960 | No comment! |
| Entertainment | £40 | £480 | I'm a cinemaholic. |
| Sport | £4 | £52 | Squash twice a week. |
| Clothes | £40 | £480 | Buying splurge every three months, often in charity shops. |
| TV licence | | £29.17 | |
| CDs | | £60 | 3–4 a year. |
| Books for pleasure | £18 | £216 | |
| Books for course | | £200 | |
| Photocopying | | £50 | |
| Holidays | | £0 | What are they? |
| Presents | | £200 | |
| Insurance | | £138 | I am dyslexic so have a computer. Theft is astronomical here, so is insurance. What goes missing? Everything. I expect to be burgled once a year and I am. |
| Newspapers | £8 | £96 | |
| Interest on Barclay Card | £5 | £60 | |
| Total | | 7690.17 | |

| Income | Per term | Per year | Comment |
|---|---|---|---|
| Grant | | £1755 | Comes in three termly lumps |
| Parental contribution | | £0 | Independent student – not expected to pay. |
| Student loan | | £1230 | Reduced rate because final year student. Taken in lump sum and invested. |
| Interest on student loan at 6.5% | | £? | Too difficult to caluclate as £50 withdrawn each week. |
| Access fund | | £80 | For hardship. |
| Interest from student loan gradually reducing at 6.5% | | | |
| Earnings term time | £229.20 | £1948.29 | Duty officer in student union bar, 20 hrs a week. |
| Earnings holiday | | £1200 | Farm work – picking lettuces planting spring onions. 12 weeks during summer. |
| Overdraft | | £1650 | |
| Student Barclay Card | | £350 | Only used in emergencies. |
| Presents at Christmas | | £10 | From an aunt. Most presents were useful. |
| Total | | £8223.29 | |

*Comment*: Everyone is in debt. Fees will definitely stop people like me getting a degree. I'm glad I'm finishing this year. Student life as a mature student is very different. Alcohol, for example, isn't a main player in my finances. There is such massive peer pressure on students to got out and drink; if I was 18 I would be the same. Compared with working it's a doddle – not having to get up until ten o'clock. For those with children it's another ball game. It was a struggle, coming back to study, I nearly gave up. Certainly being without money wasn't easy, from having a car, a flat and £15,000 a year I was counting my change, seeking out the cheapest shops, buying in bulk and rummaging through second-hand clothes. But I'm glad I've done it.

# WILL I SURVIVE MY COURSE FINANCIALLY?

A few facts about drop-outs. (Figures from the CVCP in 1994–95.)

- 21,000 students dropped out of their courses because they failed their exams.
- 32,000 students dropped out voluntarily for academic, family, and financial reasons.
- This shows a 10% rise in the number of students dropping out early.

## Thrift tips

- Don't shop on an empty stomach – it's fatal.
- Always telephone during the cheap rates – after 6pm or at weekends in the UK and after 8pm for overseas calls.
- Watch out for special coach company offers.
- Check that water rates are included in your rent.
- Look for special student nights at night clubs, theatres, cinemas.
- Check out student union shops – they buy in bulk and so give good discounts. Beer, stationery, dry cleaning, even holidays could be part of their cost-cutting service.
- Buy books second-hand.

A more recent survey by HEFC suggests:

- 4–5% of students drop out of university, but around half of those return within a year. (The number of first degree students attending university in UK in 1996–97 was 1,048,000.)
- Financial hardship was cited as an influence but was not usually the sole reason.

## So how much are you going to need to survive as a student?

£4000? £5000? £6000? £7000? £8000? Students from abroad are currently being advised that they will need at least £7000–£9000pa in London and £6000–£8000pa in other parts of the country – and that excludes books and equipment. While the NUS estimated that UK students need £5389 in London and £4232 in other parts of the country for the 38 week academic year 1997–98. You'd be lucky if you had that. In reality you're going to have to survive on what you can get and what you can earn. How much is that likely to be? Read on!

## Last word

*'I decided to take out a loan rather than take on a part-time job, because I wanted to take advantage of the opportunities at university and work towards my degree without worrying about a job. Now I think that I may have to take on a job too – the worst of both worlds.'* Scott, Maths student, Edinburgh

# 2
# WHERE WILL THE MONEY COME FROM?

## Main sources of finance for undergraduates

In this chapter we look at the main sources of finance for students embarking on higher education:

- fees
- grants
- loans
- access and hardship funds
- the banks
- funds for disabled students

and how to set about getting them.

## TWO SYSTEMS OF FUNDING

There has been a major change in the system of funding for first degree students through university starting from September/October 1998. This means that for the next four years there will be two funding systems running in our universities. To differentiate between the two systems we will talk of EXISTING STUDENTS – those who started their course on or before autumn 1997 (plus 'gap year' students who will start their course in the autumn of 1998 but had their university place confirmed by August 1997), and NEW STUDENTS – those starting in or after Autumn 1998.

## Fast facts on finance

For existing students who started their course on or before autumn 1997 and 'gap year' students whose place was confirmed by August 1997:

| | |
|---|---|
| Fees: | paid for most degree and HND students. |
| Grant: | £2225 in London, £1810 elsewhere, £1480 living at home (slightly less in Scotland), means-tested on parents' income. |
| Student loans: | £2145 in London, £1735 elsewhere, £1325 living at home – less around 27% in your final year. |
| Access funds: | random distribution depending on college; given largely to help with rent and other financial hardships. Max given £3000. |
| Study abroad: | some additional help from LEA and other schemes. |

For new students starting their course 1998–99

| | |
|---|---|
| Fees: | Max £1000pa means tested on parents income |
| Grant: | £1225 in London, £810 elsewhere, £480 living at home (slightly less in Scotland) means-tested on parents' income. Abolished from Autumn 1999. |
| Student loans: | £3145 in London, £2735 elsewhere, £2325 living at home (less in your final year). Means-tested from Autumn 1999. |
| Supplementary loan: | £250pa for those in particular financial hardship difficulty |
| Access funds: | random distribution; given largely to help with rent and other financial hardships. Max given £3000. |
| Study abroad: | some additional help from LEA and other schemes. |

*Note*: 1997 A-level students who were unable to start their course until 1998 because their grades were deemed to be inadequate, but had them raised on appeal, will be treated as existing students.

# FEES

## Who will pay my fees?

From Autumn 1998 you and your local education authority if you live in England or Wales. Otherwise the Scottish Office or the Department of Education in Northern Ireland will pay your fees, provided both you personally and your course are eligible. The student portion of fees is means-tested, so payment is affected by parental income.

## How much will I have to pay towards my fees?

Maximum £1000pa if you are a 'new student'. Nothing if you are an existing student. Amount for new students depends on parents'/family income.

## How will my fees be paid?

The part your local authority is paying will be sent direct to your university. The part you are paying will be paid direct to your university or college by you.

## Will I have to pay all my fees on the first day of university?

At the time of going to press universities were still working out how the fees were to be collected. Most will probably offer options. Some may allow you to pay on a monthly or termly basis by direct debit. Others may demand the full fee up front. While you are ultimately responsible for seeing that your fees are paid, and parents cannot be forced to contribute, your fee payment figure is based on your parents' income and it is hoped that parents will in fact pay the fees. So you should discuss with them what they are preparing to do. Those who don't pay their fees on time will be penalised, but it is unlikely that you won't be able to start your course because the fees haven't been paid. Details of how fees can be paid should be sent to you by your university before you start your course.

## Will all students living in the UK get help with fees?

No. You must have been a UK resident for the three years before your course begins. Being temporarily away from the UK – say, because your parents were working abroad – does not count as breaking your residency.

## I'm a sandwich student, will I have to pay fees during my industrial placement?

Yes. Whether it is a thick or thin sandwich placement all 'new students' will have to pay fees. Those who spend an entire year of a course on a sandwich placement at home or abroad will have to pay a maximum tuition fee of £500 (subject to means-testing). This is said to be a contribution towards the cost by the institution of administrative and pastoral arrangements relating to the placement. Where the placement is less than a full year fees of £1000 are payable.

## Many Scottish courses are a year longer than those in England. Will I have to pay another year's fees?

If you're Scottish – no. If you are English or Welsh – yes. The government has decided that Scottish students studying in Scotland on courses that are longer than the equivalent in England and Wales will not have to pay tuition fees for the final year. However, so far English and Welsh students studying in Scotland will have to pay the final year fees. If you are English or Welsh, before you decide against going to a Scottish university, check with your local education authority; it is early days in the scheme rules, regulations will be changed, and anomalies like this should be ironed out.

## Will the local authorities automatically help pay my fees for any course I take at any college?

No. Courses where assistance with fees *will* be given include: full-time (including sandwich) degree, HNC, HND, Postgraduate Certificate of Education, School-Centred Initial Teacher Training, or equivalent courses undertaken at a UK university, publicly funded college or comparable institution.

Courses where assistance with fees will *not* automatically be paid include: school-level courses such as A-levels or Scottish Highers, BTEC and SCOTVEC National Awards and City and Guilds courses, postgraduate courses (except teacher training), all part-time courses (except initial teacher training courses), correspondence and Open University courses.

## What can I do to raise funds if none of my fees are paid?

1. Apply for a discretionary grant – see next question.
2. Apply for a Career Development Loan – see page 70.

3. Apply to professional bodies, trusts, foundations, benevolent funds – see Chapter 5.

## I want to take a course where the government doesn't automatically pay part of the fees – what can I do?

Local education authorities have the power to offer 'discretionary grants'. These can cover just fees, part of fees, maintenance or part maintenance. There are no hard-and-fast rules as to how such grants are distributed, or to whom. Each local authority decides on its own policy, and each student's case is very different. In some areas discretionary grants are competitive, so your examination results could play a signicant part in your success; or you might be limited to taking a course within your local area.

## I'm on a foundation course – will I have to pay fees when I go on to do my degree?

If you started your foundation in 1997, are due to start your degree or HND course in the autumn of 1998 and it is an integral part of your degree/HND course then you will be counted as an existing student and not have to pay fees. Otherwise you will.

## Will nurses have to pay fees?

No. The NHS will provide bursaries for those on nursing and midwifery degree courses. Also for students studying  prosthetics and orthoptics, and speech language therapy, dental hygiene, dental therapy, occupational therapy, physiotherapy and radiography.

## What's my position as an overseas student?

Unless you are from the EU, or can get your own government to pay your fees, you are expected to pay them in full. Legally you can be charged higher tuition fees than UK students – so you can be thinking of: £6200 for an arts course; £8100 for science based courses; and £15,700 for clinical courses. Rates for postgraduate courses are higher (see page 155). Most universities and colleges do have a designated overseas adviser who you could contact. The rules are different for EU citizens (who pay the same fees as UK students), refugees, new immigrants and EU migrant workers.

If you are already in the UK, contact the educational enquiry service at the British Council Information Centre, Bridgewater House, 58 Whitorth Street, Manchester M1 6BB Tel: 0161 957 7755 or UKCOSA, the Council for International Education, which handles 10,000 enquiries from students a year, at 9–17 Saint Albans Place, London N1 0NX. Advisory Service Tel: 0171 354 5210 (open 1pm–4pm Mon to Fri), Fax: 0171 226 3373. Otherwise try the British Council, High Commission or Embassy in your own country.

EU students may get an award for most of their fees, but as new students they may have to pay £1000pa towards them. They will not get a grant or loan. A booklet, *Investing in the Future: Help with Tuition Fees for European Union Students*, is available.

## How will they calculate how much I must pay towards my fees?

It is based on your parents' income. As a rule of thumb, if your parents are earning less than £23,000 before tax, the whole of your fees will be paid and, for this year, you should get the full maintenance grant. If your parents have earnings before tax of £23,000–£35,000, you should get some assistance. Over that you will get no help with fees at all unless you have brothers or sisters also at university, but you may still get some grant for 1998.  Remember, if you are an existing or 1997 gap year student, you will not have to pay any fees throughout your course. For more details keep reading.

## How will I know how much I must pay towards my fees?

Once your family income has been assessed, your LEA will let you know. They will also tell your university.

## Will student fees go up?

The government has said that the fees paid by students are, and I quote, 'unlikely to go up more than the rate of inflation' which probably means

YES. But when they will be reviewed and exactly by how much they will be increased is anyone's guess.

# MAINTENANCE GRANTS

## What is a maintenance grant?

A maintenance grant is the money paid to students by their local authority to live on while they are studying.

## Does every student get one?

No. They are means-tested, generally on your parents' income.

## Are maintenance grants really being abolished?

Yes, but in stages. Students who start their course in September/October 1998 will be eligible for a reduced maintenance grant for one year only. From autumn 1999 it will be abolished for you and all new students. For existing students who started their course in or before 1997 and 1997 gap year students grants will continue right up to the end of their course.

## Is it right or is it wrong?

This book does not set out to argue the rights and wrongs of the students' situation, its function is to provide information. Not surprisingly, however, our research revealed strong feelings among students about the cut in grants. Here are a few of their more printable comments:

*'It's ridiculous, the grants are to be slashed and I think anybody intending to enter higher education should be aware of the difficulty of surviving. Don't rely on finding part-time work – it is EXTREMELY difficult and very competitive.' (Leeds)*

*'This government appears to be preventing the poor from being educated, creating yet again an educated elite.' (Manchester)*

'*More and more students are dropping out of uni due to student financial hardship. Not in one's wildest imagination can you get enough to live on; you'd be better off on the dole.*' *(Manchester)*

'*Lack of parental contribution already makes life impossible. I live on half what I should. Books need subsidising.*' *(Brunel University)*

'*University – it's more a big survival struggle than an academic challenge.*' *(Brunel University)*

**Final word**

'*Help I'm skint; I have just £8 to last two terms.*' *(Manchester)*

**What the government said:**

'*The new system will mean that universities and colleges have more money to improve standards.*'

'*On average, a graduate earns 20% more than someone without a degree within about 10 years of graduation. Over a working lifetime, that will make a big difference in their income.*'

# What is the full maintenance grant for existing students?

| 1998–99 | England/Wales N. Ireland | Scotland |
|---|---|---|
| Living away from home and studying in London | £2225 | £2145 |
| Living away from home and studying outside London | £1810 | £1735 |
| Living at home | £1480 | £1325 |

# What is the full maintenance grant for new students?

| 1998–99 | England/Wales N. Ireland | Scotland |
|---|---|---|
| Living away from home and studying in London | £1225 | £1145 |
| Living away from home and studying outside London | £810 | £735 |
| Living at home | £480 | £325 |

## Why is the grant for new students £1000 less?

Because the government is paying up to £1000 towards their fees.

## How will new students manage – they will be £1000 less well off?

Don't panic. To compensate for the cut in grants, the loan for new students will be £1000 more. And when the grant is abolished next year the loan will go up again for new students to cover this loss. For details on loans keep reading.

## Why are Scottish grants lower?

Because the full cost of travelling expenses is not included. Scottish students who receive a maintenance grant can claim for travelling expenses over a certain amount. The current figure is £70 but this can change. There are of course certain restrictions, like using the cheapest form of transport, but it's well worth applying, especially if your university is a long way from home.

## Will I get a grant?

Getting money out of anyone is never easy, and the government is no exception. The government estimates that for 1998–99, the percentage of students receiving maintenance and/or fees is as follows.

|                                | England/Wales | Scotland |
|--------------------------------|---------------|----------|
| Nil maintenance/fees           | 33.3%         | 20%      |
| Some maintenance/some fees     | 33.3%         | 40%      |
| Full maintenance/fees          | 33.3%         | 40%      |

How much a student is entitled to depends on how much their parents (or spouse) earn, and remember: they consider your parents' joint income.

## My parents are divorced, which one will be liable for contributions?

In 1998–99 as now, your local education authority will decide which parent's income is to be used for assessment contributions. This, however, is being reviewed for 1999–2000.

## How do they calculate how much grant and fees I am entitled to?

The actual calculation of how much your parents are expected to contribute towards your fees and maintenance – if any – is very complex, and based on their 'residual income': that means what's left after essential expenses have been deducted.

So what are essential expenses? It works like this. The LEA takes your parents' gross income and then subtracts allowances for things like interest payments (mortgage up to £30,000), dependants (including grandparents or other adults allowance £2140, pension schemes, life assurance, and superannuation payments that qualify for tax relief. You also get £75 reduction on parental contribution for each dependent child and in certain circumstances, such as if a parent is disabled, you can claim up to £1680 for domestic help.

## But how does it work?

As a rule of thumb, a parental total income of about £23,000 equates to a residual income of about £16,945, which means:

- **New students:** your parents would have to make no contribution at all, so you would get the £1000 fees paid and a grant of £1225 if studying in London and £810 if studying elsewhere.
- **Existing students:** grant of £2225 studying in London, £1810 elsewhere. Parents' contribution towards your maintenance £0.

If your parents gross income was around £27,000 and their residual income was assessed at, say, £20,000:

- **New students:** your parents' would contribute just £280 towards your fees. You would then get £720 of your fees paid by your LEA and for the year 1998–99 receive a grant of £1225 if studying in London and £810 is studying elsewhere.
- **Existing students:** grant of £1945 studying in London, £1530 elsewhere. Parents' contribution towards your maintenance £280.

Again, as a rule of thumb, a total income of £35,000 equates to a residual income of around £27,116 so:

- **New students:** your parents would have to pay the full £1000 fees, but in the year 1998–99 you would still get the grant of £1225 if studying in London and £810 if studying elsewhere.
- **Existing students:** grant of £1225 in London and £810 elsewhere. Parents' contribution towards your maintenance: £1000.

If your parents' residual income was assessed at £30,000, which means their gross income could be over £38,000:

- **New students:** parents would be expected to pay all your fees of £1000 and £313 towards your maintenance and for this year you would still get a grant of £912 in London and £497 if studying elsewhere.
- **Existing students:** grant of £912 in London and £497 if studying elsewhere. Parents contribution towards your maintenance £1313.

Remember these are just examples, so don't take them too literally. Calculating residual income is complex and depends very much on personal circumstances, how many dependants in the family and so on.

The local authority generally looks at your parents' last year's income. But if this has suddenly taken a tumble your parents can always ask to be assessed on their current earnings.

## What happens if my parents are not prepared to divulge their income?

Then you will get no grant from the local authority and no help with fees. You may also find when loans are means-tested from Autumn 1999 that you may not be able to take out the full amount you are entitled to.

## To claim a full grant and full fees how little must my parents earn?

To claim a full grant, your parents must have a combined residual income of less than £16,945 (1998–99 figures).

## To get any grant or help with fees what is the maximum my parents can earn?

If you are the only child in the family in higher education living away from home, the cut-off point for your parents' residual income is between £30,000 and £35,000, depending on where you are intending to study and live. But remember, it is residual income, so actual earnings might be substantially more.

## What if I have a brother or sister who also wants a grant?

If there are several children in the family in higher education, all claiming maintenance and fees, the parents' residual income can be much higher, as the parental contribution is divided proportionately between the children. For example, if there were two students in one family, both attending a college outside London, their combined support could be £3620. As you can see from the chart (opposite), the parents' residual income would need to be around £45,000, and their gross income substantially more, before they got no help at all.

## Does the parental contribution ever change?

Yes. The threshold at which parents begin to contribute towards maintenance and fees was raised in 1998 from a residual parental income of

## Grant calculation chart

**Contribution scale for students entering higher education after September 1998**

| Parents' residual income | Parents' contribution |
|---|---|
| £ | £ |
| 0–16,944 | nil |
| 16,945 | 45 |
| 20,000 | 280 |
| 30,000 | 1313 |
| 40,000 | 2603 |
| 50,000 | 3934 |
| 60,000 | 5269 |
| 66,430 or more | 6125 |

Contributions are calculated as follows:

| Residual income | |
|---|---|
| From £16,945 to £21,659 | £1 in £13.00 |
| From 21,660 to £31,839 | £1 in  £9.20 |
| From £31,840 | £1 in  £7.50 |

£16,450 to £16,945, and the rest of the scale was adjusted accordingly. At the same time, however, students fees have been introduced and the grant for existing students has been increased by just over £50. So, where does that leave parents, and you?

*Note to parents*: No parent is *expected* to contribute more than the maximum grant plus the cost of fees for each student, however high their income. Whether your son or daughter is being funded under the new or old scheme, your *expected* contribution is the same.

## What if my mum or dad is made redundant?

If your parents' income suddenly drops, then your grant/fees entitlement will need to be recalculated, and you should contact your local education authority, or Awards Branch immediately.

A cautionary tale of Catch 22

> *'My grant does not cover my rent; my parents are both unemployed. If I don't get a job in term time I get into debt, but if I do it diminishes my course work. OK, you say, work in the holidays. If I go home during the holidays and work I have to pay part of my parents' council house rent*

*because I am classified as the 'breadwinner', which vexes and perplexes me and them. This discourages me from going home. Result, my parents and I are growing further apart'.* John, English/Management student, Aberdeen

## If my parents can't afford to or won't pay their share of my maintenance and fees, is there anything I can do?

No. There is no way that parents can be made to pay their contribution towards your maintenance and fees, and the local authorities will not make up the difference. The National Union of Students estimated that over a third of students find that their parents do not pay their full contribution, but no recent study has been done. In Austria parents are taken to court if they don't pay their share of the means-tested grant, but not in the UK. However, early in 1998 a student in Scotland did take his mother to court and she was ordered to pay something towards his maintenance. But this is an exception – so far! And, contrary to student mythology, it is no good getting your parents to write to your local authority saying they have kicked their student child out and are no longer giving them house room, in the hope of getting a full grant. A spokeswoman at the DfEE assured us: *'We are up to that one. The government has left no loopholes unclosed. Nice try!'*

It can come as rather a shock to parents when they discover just how much they are expected to fork out, especially if the student's course covers four years. If you get no LEA assistance, you could be thinking in terms of £5500–£9000.

*'Education had always been free for us, and we thought when our daughter went to university things wouldn't be any different. So it came as something of a body blow when, a few weeks before she left for the North, we discovered she would get no help at all and we were going to have to dig deep and find the full maintenance contribution, around £750 a term. By then it was too late to start thinking of universities closer to home.'* (Helen Wolf, London)

## Are there any circumstances where my parents would not be expected to contribute towards my maintenance and fees?

Yes – if you:

- are 25 or over
- have been married for at least two years
- have been supporting yourself for three years
- are an orphan
- are in care.

## I want to go to a university in my home town, but don't want to live with my parents – can I get the full financial package?

Students living at home are eligible for reduced financial support only. If your home is within ten miles of your chosen university or college then your local education authority will see no need for you to live in lodgings, even if you do, and usually only give the lower 'home rate' allowance. However, if you can make a good case for the need to live away from home, such as transport problems or personal health reasons, then you can appeal.

## I'm thinking of getting married – will it affect my maintenance/fees entitlements?

Not immediately. But if you have been married for over two years, your partner, provided he or she is earning enough, will be asked to pay up. The spouse's contribution starts at a lower rate of residual income than for parents, and is significantly higher – see the chart on page 46. The reason given by the DfEE for this obvious spouse discrimination is that your partner is likely to gain more from your higher education than your parents. It has a kind of logic. Still, we understand that the system is under review.

| Spouse's residual income | Spouse's contribution |
|---|---|
| £ | £ |
| 13,405 | 10 |
| 15,000 | 172 |
| 20,000 | 682 |
| 30,000 | 2034 |
| 40,000 | 3752 |
| 50,000 | 5537 |
| 53,289 or more | 6125 |
| | |
| Contributions are calculated as follows: | |
| From £13,405 to £21,664 | £1 in £9.80 |
| From £21,665 to £31,834 | £1 in £7.05 |
| From £31,835 | £1 in £5.60 |

## Will I get financial support if I take a paramedical course?

Yes, but from a different source – you won't have to pay fees and you will get a bursary. The health authorities provide awards for students on recognised courses; these include occupational therapy, physiotherapy, radiography, orthoptics, dental hygiene, dental therapy. The awards are worked out in a similar way to students attending universities, so the information in the book is relevant. If your bursary is means-tested you may also be able to apply for a loan.

> Training for Nurses – for information on bursaries for Project 2000 nurse education and training courses, nursing and midwifery degree courses contact your local regional office of the NHS Executive or your Health Department in Scotland, Wales or Northern Ireland.

## I'm an overseas student, can I get a grant or help with my fees?

No. Even students from the EU classified as 'home' students as far as basic fees are concerned are generally not eligible for any financial assistance with student fees contribution or a loan.

## When should I apply for financial assistance?

**England/Wales/Northern Ireland:** As soon as possible. Application forms should be available from your school, otherwise from your local education authority. You do not need to wait to be accepted by a university or college to apply.

**Scotland:** When you receive an unconditional offer from a university or college. Application forms are available from your school and Awards Branch from April for courses starting in the autumn.

## What is the maintenance grant meant to go towards?

Lodgings, food, books, pocket money, travel.

**Note:** in Scotland the grant is slightly less, as it covers only travel up to £70. Excess travel costs may be claimed using Form AB4, available from your university or college.

## My academic year is longer than at most colleges – can I claim any extra money from my local authority?

Yes. If your course is longer than 30 weeks 3 days in any year (25 weeks 3 days at Oxford and Cambridge), you can claim extra from your local authority. The full rates in 1998–99 are:

| | |
|---|---|
| London | £82.20 |
| Elsewhere | £61.60 |
| Living at home | £43.15 |

If your course year is 45 weeks or longer, you will receive a grant based on 52 weeks.

## Are there any other allowances I could apply for?

Yes.

1. **Travelling expenses** *England, Wales and Northern Ireland:* the first £256 of any travelling expenses if you live at home, and £166 if you live away, must be met from your grant. Above that you can claim for certain

expenses: ie if you are disabled; attending another establishment as part of a medical or dental course; attending an institution abroad as part of your course.

*Scotland:* if living away from home, three return journeys per year to your place of study can be claimed for plus additional term-time travel to and from your institution. (This does not include students whose parents live outside the UK.) The first £70 of claim will be disregarded. Only the most economical fares will be allowed. Living at parental home: maximum paid £3 per day plus £495. Mature students with dependants: maximum paid £3 per day plus £635 (1997–98 figures). If the Scots look as if they are having things much better, remember their grants are lower.

2. **Two homes allowance** Maintaining a home other than the home you live in to attend the course – £700.

3. **Dependants**

| | |
|---|---|
| Spouse/ | £2025 max |
| Other adults | |
| Children depending on | |
| age and circumstances | £425 to £2025 |

# If I work part-time, will it affect my student financial package?

No. Students can work during their course – ie undertake vacation work – and the money earned will not be considered when their grant is calculated. However, sandwich course students who undertake a year's *paid* industrial training will not receive a grant during that year but may receive assistance with fees, depending on family income. It is estimated that over half of all students work during the vacation and, according to a recent survey by the NUS, 30% during term time.

# Is there any kind of income that could affect my financial package?

Yes. If you received more than:

- £3865 from a scholarship or sponsorship, or from your employer
- £1810 from a trust income

- £3030 from a pension, except a disability pension
- £800 from other sources (this does not include vacation work).

## If I get a grant how will it be paid?

Maintenance grants are paid in three termly instalments. A cheque is sent to your university or college for collection at the beginning of each term. You will be told beforehand how much to expect.

## Panic! My maintenance cheque hasn't arrived!

It happens – not that often, but it can be dramatic when it does. In an ideal world your cheque should be waiting for you when you arrive at your university or college, but things can go wrong.

Typical reasons we discovered:

- the local authority computers went down, so the cheques didn't get out on time
- local authorities were behind with their workload
- student applied late for a grant, so the amount of the grant had not been assessed
- the university lost the cheque.

Whatever the reason, it doesn't help the destitute students to eat, so . . .

## What can I do if my grant doesn't come?

- **Try the bank:** If you already have a bank account, the bank may help you out with a loan – talk to the Student Advisor at the campus or local branch. This, of course, is no help to the first-year student who needs a grant cheque to open a bank account.

- **Try your LEA:** If the hold-up is caused because your grant allocation is still being calculated, you can ask your local authority for a provisional payment.

- **Try your college:** Ask your college for temporary help. Most institutions have what's called a hardship fund set up to cover just this kind of eventuality.

- **Try Access:** Finally, there are the Access Funds which have been set up to help students. Full details are given on page 71.

## Cash crisis notes

- As you will not be able to bank your maintenance grant until you have arrived at your university or college, you will need to have some money of your own to get yourself there, and possibly to maintain yourself until the cheque is cleared. Check out the cost of train fares.

- If you are living in halls of residence, your college will probably be sympathetic if your cheque hasn't arrived and will wait until it does. But don't be too sure about this – check it out. Some colleges will add a penalty to the bills of students who don't pay up on time. And if you run out of money and can't pay your bill at all, you will not be allowed to re-register for the next academic year; or if it's your final year, you will not get your degree until the bill is paid.

- If you are living in rented accommodation, you can expect no leniency. Landlords expect to be paid on the dot, usually ask for rent in advance and may request an additional deposit. You will need funds to cover this.

- Check with your university before you arrive about the arrangement for paying your fee contribution. You may need a lot of money up front.

- **Friends?** They may well take pity on you when it comes to socialising, buying you the odd drink, but it is rarely a good idea to borrow from friends.

## What will happen if I drop out of my course?

You may have to repay some of your award to your LEA.

## I have to spend part of my course studying abroad – will I get a top up grant?

Yes. Living costs in different countries vary, so your financial entitlements are adjusted to cover this. There are four categories:

- **Highest-cost countries**: these include Denmark, Finland, Iceland, Japan, Norway, Sweden, Switzerland and Taiwan.

- **Higher-cost countries**: these include Austria, Belgium, France, Germany, Hong Kong, Israel, Korea, Luxembourg, The Netherlands and Russia plus other countries previously in the USSR.

- **High-cost countries**: Australia, Canada, Greece, Indonesia, Republic of Ireland, Italy, New Zealand, the USA and Spain.

- **All other countries.**

While students studying in the 'all other countries' category will receive the normal funding for students, those visiting the high-cost to highest-cost countries can apply for additional funding for the year. The full rates for 1998–99 for England and Wales are:

|  | Existing students | New students |
|---|---|---|
| Highest-cost countries: | £3410 | £2410 |
| Higher-cost countries: | £2865 | £1865 |
| High-cost countries: | £2325 | £1325 |
| All other countries: | £1810 | £810 |

From autumn 1999, new students will probably find it's their loan that is increased as there will be no grant. But this had not yet been resolved when this edition went to press.

## My course abroad is longer than my course in the UK – can I get more money?

Yes. The rates given here are worked out on a year of only 30 weeks 3 days (25 weeks 3 days for Oxbridge). If you need to stay longer, you can claim more. Rates for 1998–99 per week are:

| | |
|---|---|
| Highest-cost countries: | £115.05 |
| Higher-cost countries: | £97.50 |
| High-cost countries: | £79.85 |
| All other countries: | £62.15 |

*'Students who have a compulsory study period abroad can get into serious financial difficulties. Nobody warns you of the cost of this before you choose a course such as European studies and modern languages.'* Gillian, 3rd year French and Russian student

## It's going to cost me a lot more to fly to Tokyo than to take a train to Leeds – can I get any help with travel?

Yes, but you won't get full reimbursement. Your grant already includes some travel element (£166 for full grant in England, Wales and Northern Ireland, £70 Scotland), and this will be taken into consideration in calculating how much you receive. It is probably best to let your local authority calculate what you are entitled to. Remember when putting in for costs to give all the facts – that journey from your home to the airport costs something too.

**Note to higher-earning parents:** While your earnings might disqualify your son or daughter from claiming any maintenance while they are based in this country, if they are studying in one of the high-cost countries you may qualify for some help. This is not spelt out in the Department for Education and Employment leaflet, so check the figures with your local authority. It's always worth a try.

## Is there any other help for students who want to study abroad?

Three organisations have been set up to assist students wanting to study in the EU:

SOCRATES–ERASMUS, the European Community Action Scheme for the Mobility of University Students, is designed to encourage greater cooperation between universities and other higher educational institutions in Europe. Under this scheme, students taking courses, including foreign languages, in other European countries may be given a grant towards extra expenses while studying abroad for a period of 3–12 months. These could include travel expenses, language courses, or living and accommodation costs.

LEONARDO da VINCI provides opportunities for university students and recent graduates to undertake periods of vocational training of up to 12 months with organisations in other member states – placements are largely technology based. While individual employers will provide any salary, the Leonardo scheme can make a contribution towards language tuition and expenses.

## Who to contact

Funding from these organisations is arranged mainly through your university or college. They should have full information and should, therefore, be your first point of call. Otherwise contact The European Commission – see page 54 for the address.

## What happens if I get sick while studying abroad?

Don't wait until you get sick, take out health insurance cover before you go. (See details under travel insurance on page 112.) Your local authority will probably reimburse the costs of health insurance providing they consider it 'economical'. Check out the situation with them first or ask for advice from your university before you take out any insurance cover. Remember, above everything else, to hold on to your receipts. Without those you are unlikely to get reimbursement from your local authority.

## Where can I find out more about grants and fees?

Full information about grants is given in the following free booklets, which you would be well advised to get and study.

For students in England and Wales:
*Financial Support for Students: A guide to grants, loans and fees in higher education*
Department for Education and Employment, Publications Centre, PO Box 505, Sudbury, Suffolk CO10 6AU. Tel: 0800 731 9133; e-mail: info@dfee.gov.uk.

For students in Scotland:
*Student Fees and Grants in Scotland*, available from any Scottish University. In case of difficulty, contact the Scottish Office Education Department, Gyleview House, 3 Redheughs Rigg, South Gyle, Edinburgh EH12 9HH. For booklet tel: 0131 244 8075; Fax: 0131 244 5887. General Enquiries: 0131 244 5823.

For students in Northern Ireland:
*Grants and loans to Students*, Student Support Branch, Department of Education for Northern Ireland, Rathgael House, Balloo Road, Bangor, Co. Down BT19 7PR. Tel: 01247 279279; Fax: 01247 279100.

For Welsh speaking students:
  Welsh Office Education Department, FHE1 Division, 4th Floor, Cathays Park, Cardiff, CF1 3NQ. Tel: 01222 825831; Fax: 01222 825823.

UK SOCRATES–ERASMUS Council, University of Kent, Canterbury CT2 7PD. Tel: 01227 762712.

LEONARDO da VINCI, check with your university or college.

THE EUROPEAN CHOICE – *A Guide to Opportunities for Higher Education in Europe*, available free from the DfEE Publications Centre, PO Box 505, Sudbury, Suffolk CO10 6AU. Tel: 0845 6022260.

THE EUROPEAN COMMISSION – London Office: 8 Storey's Gate, London SW1P 3AT. Tel: 0171 973 1992. Ask for their free booklet: *Funding from the European Union*.

# LOANS

## How on earth are students expected to manage if they abolish the maintenance grant?

Student loans. For some years now the grant has only been half the story. In the autumn of 1990 the student loan was introduced, and with it a new attitude in this country to the financing of students through higher education. Now we are facing yet another funding revolution with the loan being the main source of maintenance funding for students. If the idea of being in debt to the tune of possibly £10,000 or more when you leave university fills you with horror (and why shouldn't it) read on, because things aren't quite as gloomy as they seem.

## The student loan – what are the 'real' facts?

When first introduced the newspapers were full of stories about the rights and wrongs of the Student Loans Scheme. Some thought that education in this country should be completely free; others that students should contribute to their education. There were forceful arguments on both sides and people are still arguing. It was thought at the time student numbers would plummet. But they didn't. In fact, they continued to rise. So what will be the effect of the new system?

Whatever your views, and whether you like the idea or not of funding yourself through university, if you are a student just starting on higher education in this country you will probably end up having a hefty loan. In the first year of the student loan scheme, around £70 million was paid out to fund some 180,000 students. In 1997, £878 million was paid out to 590,000 students. There is no doubt the student loan scheme is now an integral part of student finance, and student life.

Compared with your predecessors' situation, it's tough. But students are reluctantly learning to live with debt.

## Is it right or wrong?

When the Student Loan Scheme was first introduced obviously it caused a lot of controversy as shown by these quotes from students at the University of Westminster on a BBC Radio 4 programme:

*'I really didn't want to take out a loan and hung out to the end, but I needed to clear my overdraft. So I had to eat my words and take one out anyway.'*

*'If you take out a loan in your first year, second year and third year, by the time you leave you have an enormous debt to pay off and it is a bit of a deterrent to students to come to university. If you drop out of your course halfway through and you end up with an enormous debt and no degree, you're going to be in a bit of a state.'*

*'It's quite a frightening thought when you're only 20 years old to say: "Oh, I'm borrowing all this money – what chance have I got of ever paying it back?"'*

*'I should be concentrating on finishing off my course and looking towards my career. As it stands, I have to worry about the pressures of money and having a court summons brought up against me for debts and suchlike. It is very difficult to concentrate sometimes.'* (A 21-year-old third-year student who had failed to pay his credit card bill and had debts mounting to £3000)

While some students interviewed thought it was only fair that they should partly fund themselves rather than place the burden on the shoulders of the state, others thought the government was going the wrong way about attracting more people into higher education.

Today's students are much more reconciled to the situation of being in debt, as a survey carried out by Barclays Bank shows:

| *Attitude to debt by final year students:* | 1994 | 1995 | 1997 |
|---|---|---|---|
| Worried | 11% | 7% | 7% |
| Concerned | 9% | 10% | 13% |
| Angry | 26% | 18% | 10% |
| Resigned | 37% | 33% | 34% |
| Pleased not to have much loan | 17% | 32% | 23% |
| Unconcerned | | | 13% |

However, students who took part in the *Students' Money Matters* research had this to say:

> *'No matter how careful you are with money you will still be in debt, and having £3000 debt hanging over you isn't the best way to start a career.'* Brunel University

> *'We need more money not less! It's an outrage.'* Robert Gordon University, Aberdeen

> *'It's exceedingly difficult trying to maintain a reasonable standard of life – student finance is crap.'* York University

> *'Don't let the lack of finances deter you from going to university.'* La Sainte Union

> *'If I can't find a job in the vacations, I have a problem affording to eat.'* University of Central England

> *'Depression is a problem that hits everyone who lives on a tight budget.'* Manchester University

There are other students who take a different view:

> *'Generally studying is an indulgent luxury which improves prospects and so people should take as much responsibility as possible.'* Law Student, Manchester

> *'If a student is prepared to work part-time finance is not a problem – it depends on the student's attitude.'* Social Science student, Bradford

> *'Students with massive debts generally spend too much time indulging in the pubs and curry houses.'* Electronic and Electrical Engineering student, Bradford

> *'Get rid of grants! Give us realistic student loan amounts – what we get is a joke. I don't want handouts, just the opportunity to borrow.'* Politics, Philosophy, Economics student, Oxford

*'Most students don't mind the thought of paying back money once they are earning.'* Human Sciences student, Oxford

This book does not set out to argue the rights and wrongs of how students are financed through higher education – we leave that to others. Our aim is to give you hard information on how to juggle your finances and tap every source available so that you can cope in the current economic climate.

# HOW DO BRITAIN'S STUDENTS FARE COMPARED WITH STUDENTS IN OTHER COUNTRIES?

Judge for yourself. When it comes to funding students through higher education, it would seem that no country has found the perfect solution: some countries provide loans, others grants, and the rest a combination of both – and the permutations are endless.

If you are looking for a common approach from our continental neighbours, forget it. Almost all students in The Netherlands get assistance, while in France hardly any do. When it comes to levels of loans available, there are big differences too: a student in Norway can pick up over three times more than a student in Denmark, which may seem hard until you realise the Danish student is cushioned by a generous grant.

To make things worse, nobody seems to be satisfied, so just when you are beginning to get systems sorted out, countries will change things. Germany abolished grants in favour of loans in 1984, but is now thinking of bringing them back in some kind of dual system.

Sweden has been tinkering with its system continually for 25 years, moving from a grants system to an almost entirely loans system, and now swinging back in favour of grants again. Recently it has increased the grant portion of the total amount paid out to students to around 28%. Even so, most students graduate with a massive debt. Around £10,000 is common. For those studying medicine or engineering it will be considerably more.

In Australia, there is a mix between means-tested grants and loans, similar to here, but all students are required to pay back 23% of their tuition costs either up front on enrolment, when they get a 25% discount, or after graduation, when a pay-back rate is set depending on income. So looking for the differences in systems is easier than seeking comparisons, as you'll see from the six systems reviewed below.

**France:** Fees are paid by the government, but all students must pay a registration fee of up to £150 a year. Most students support themselves, as grants are not widely available. 'Hardship' students can get help with living expenses, based on parental income and the number claiming support is increasing, but this funding can be withdrawn if performance is not satisfactory. Loans are given only in extreme circumstances. There is high public funding on subsidised food and accommodation. Maintenance grants can also be paid while at school to low income families.

**Germany:** Fees are covered by the state and students can attend the university of their choice, even changing institution at will during courses. In West Germany during most of the 1980s the state provided interest-free long-term loans for needy students (around 33%). However, since 1990 financial assistance has been on a fifty–fifty basis: half grant and half loan which is means-tested. The loan repayment begins five years after graduation and extends over 20 years. East Germany has now been brought in line with West. The majority of students need part-time work to help finance themselves.

**Denmark:** Students in Denmark are considered independent at the age of 18 and so all are eligible for a grant if they go to college. This ranges from £100 a month for those living at home to £320 a month for those in lodgings, with the additional option of a loan of around £160 a month available. Interest rates on government loans are 4% during the course and currently 4.5% once qualified. While the cost of living in Denmark is slightly higher than in the UK, students can just about manage on the grant, providing they don't party every night.

**Belgium:** All grants are means-tested on parents' income, but those who receive a full grant should find it enough to live on. There is no system of loans so Belgian students do not generally get into debt. Belgium is a small country so many students live at home and those that live away generally go home at weekends. Accommodation costs are not as expensive as in the UK. All students have to pay an enrolment fee (which differs between university and non-university establishments) for their course and if they don't get a grant parents have to pay this. Courses are generally longer than in the UK: 2–3 years for non degree courses, 4–5 for degrees.

**Sweden:** A mix of grants and loans provided by the state. Assistance is means-tested but only on the student's own income. Parents' or spouse's income is not taken into account. The non-repayable grant is about 38% of the total amount (currently about £147 a month), with the rest (£877 approx a month) given as a loan. Interest is fixed annually by the government and in 1997 was 6%. 'Payback' is set at 4% of income with repayments beginning within six months of finishing the course. At least 74% of students who study in Sweden have a loan and 80% of those who study abroad. In the main, Swedish students are better off than their counterparts in the UK, but their debts are massive.

**America:** Students are responsible for paying both their fees and living expenses. These vary enormously depending on individual colleges and whether they are state or privately run. Tuition fees range from around $3000 to $14000 at a state-supported institution, to $8000–$22,000 for a private institution. On top of that you have living costs which could add another $4000–$14,000 to your bill each 9-month academic year (1995–96 figures). Some financial aid is granted, but in most institutions it is on academic merit and full scholarships are rare. Because of this, students often have jobs during term time and work their way through college. The long summer break is designed so that students can earn enough money to pay for the academic year ahead. Other forms of funding include scholarships for special talents such as athletics and the performing arts. Special loans are available to all students. Many universities in the USA are vast and can resemble small cities with their own post office, grocery stores and shopping centres; they can dominate the local community and its economy.

# HOW STUDENT LOANS WORK: THE FACTS

## Who can get a loan?

The loans are intended largely for students undertaking full-time first degree or Diploma of Higher Education courses at universities or colleges of higher education. There are a few anomalies, such as the Diploma in Social Work and certain paramedical courses, so it is always worth checking.

## Can overseas students get a loan?

The short answer is no. You will need to have met certain residency criteria.

# How much can I borrow?

The loan is reviewed annually and is dependent on where you are studying. With two funding systems for students now running in our universities, what you can borrow will also depend on when you became a student. The rates for 1998–99 for existing students who started their course on or before autumn 1997 are:

|  | *full year* | *final year* |
|---|---|---|
| Students living away from home and studying in London | £2,145 | £1,565 |
| Other locations | £1,735 | £1,265 |
| Students living at home | £1,325 | £970 |

For new students starting their course in autumn 1998:

|  | *full year* | *final year* |
|---|---|---|
| Students living away from home and studying in London | £3145 | £2565 |
| Other locations | £2735 | £2265 |
| Students living at home | £2325 | £1970 |

Every year a new rate is fixed, depending on inflation. See next question.

---

Total student resources from grants and loans for existing students 1998–99

| Students living away from home and studying |  | Basic grant | Loan | Total |
|---|---|---|---|---|
| London | full year | £2225 | £2145 | £4370 |
|  | final year | £2225 | £1565 | £3790 |
| Other locations | full year | £1810 | £1735 | £3545 |
|  | final year | £1810 | £1265 | £3075 |
| Students living at home | full year | £1480 | £1325 | £2805 |
|  | final year | £1480 | £970 | £2350 |

Total student resources from grants and loans for 'new students' in 1998–99

| Students living away from and studying |  | Basic grant | Loan | Total |
|---|---|---|---|---|
| London | full year | £1225 | £3145 | £4370 |
|  | final year | £1225 | £2565 | £3790 |
| Other locations | full year | £810 | £2735 | £3545 |
|  | final year | £810 | £2665 | £3075 |
| Students living at home | full year | £480 | £2325 | £2805 |
|  | final year | £480 | £1970 | £2350 |

## Why are new students loans so much higher than existing students?

This is because £1000 of the maintenance grant now goes towards paying fees. Compare the totals columns in the box on the previous page and you will see the funds available to 'existing students' and 'new students' are the same, they just come from different sources.

## What will I get in Autumn 1999 when maintenance grants are abolished?

When maintenance grants are abolished students who started their course on or after Autumn 1998 will find the loan available to them has been increased to cover this amount. While the actual figure has not yet been announced, it will be similar to the total amount available to you this year, ie £4370 if studying in London and £3545 if studying elsewhere plus something to cover for inflation. So you will be no less well off than this year, just building up a greater debt.

## Why are the rates lower for the final year?

Because they do not cover the summer vacation. You are expected to be working by then, or can draw Social Security. However, if your final year lasts 40 weeks or more you can get a loan at the full rate. This is often the case for students on 'accelerated' degree courses.

## Are loans means-tested?

They have not been until now, and will not be until autumn 1999. But when the maintenance grant is abolished and loans for 'new students' are increased to compensate for that, then the loan will be means-tested for 'new students' along with the means-testing for paying fees. The situation will not alter for existing students.

## I'm studying abroad – can I get a loan?

Yes. If you study or work abroad for a full year as part of your course you are eligible for the 'elsewhere' locations rate. If you are normally based at

a London college and away for less than a year, you can apply for the
higher rate.

## When can I apply for a loan?

Once you are attending a higher education course you can apply for a
loan. You can reapply each year once the autumn term has started.
Applications can be made at any time during the academic year.
However, there are two important dates to remember:

- **30 June**: colleges are not obliged to certify your eligibility for a loan
  after this date, and you do need that certi-cation to get a loan.
- **31 July**: loans will not be issued after this date.

## When is the best time to take out a student loan?

There are three options:

1. When you need it.
2. As late as possible because it's index-linked to inflation (see page 64
   for explanation).
3. As soon as possible. We hear some financially astute students are
   taking out their student loan, even if they don't need it, and investing
   it in a good interest-paying account with a bank or building society.
   These generally pay more than the inflation rate. Make sure you know
   what you are doing. Check out interest rates first. Ensure you can get
   at your money quickly and easily if you are likely to need it – some of
   the high interest rate accounts give limited access.

Postgraduates are not entitled to a student loan. So if as an undergraduate you do not need the loan or all of the loan now, but are thinking
of going on to do a postgraduate course, it might be worth your while
taking out the student loan and investing it, so the money is there to help
you through your postgraduate studies later on. If you are not a financial
whizz-kid, take advice. The student loan is a really cheap way of
borrowing money but you don't want to build up debt unnecessarily.

*'Because I had sponsorship, had worked for a year before uni and had a
Saturday job, I didn't need a student loan, but I took it out anyway, and
put it in a good building society account, just in case I wanted to go on to do
further study. As it is, my sponsor has offered me a job that's too good to
turn down, so I won't need it, but it was nice to have that 'security' cushion*

*there. I haven't checked it out yet, but I think the loan has actually made me money; at least it hasn't cost me anything, which has to be good.'* Third year student

## How do I get a loan?

The forms needed to apply for a loan are available from your university or college. An adviser will probably also help you to fill them in. If you were born in the UK you will need your birth or adoption certificate or certified copy. If you were born abroad you should bring your passport, or a letter or document which gives details of your place and date of birth. Your bank or building society account number is also needed.

## Do I have to take out the whole amount?

No. You can take out however much you want up to the maximum for that year, but you can make only one application a year. So if you do not apply for the full amount, you *cannot* apply for the rest later.

## When will I get the money?

It should be paid into your bank or building society account within 21 days of your application arriving at the loans company, and all the required information being supplied.

## Will the loan be paid all at once in a lump sum?

If you are an existing student you can choose to have your loan paid in one lump sum or in two or three instalments. Loans for new students will be paid in termly instalments – you have no choice.

## Who runs the scheme?

A government-owned Student Loans Company has been set up to administer the loans scheme. It is based in Glasgow.

# THE SYSTEM FOR EXISTING STUDENTS

## When do I have to pay back the money?

You can start paying the money back as soon as you like, but you won't be asked to start repaying your loan until the April after you complete or leave your course, and then only if your income is 85% of national average earnings, which at the moment is about £16,488. Each year the government sets a level of monthly income under which you can put off repayments. For 1997–98 it was set at £1374.

## Is the loan interest-free?

You will have to pay back more than you borrowed in actual money on the table, although not in real terms so, the answer is 'yes and no'. Confused? This is how it works.

The amount you borrow is index-linked to inflation. So if, for example, you borrowed £2085 in the first year of a three-year course and the annual inflation rate was 2.6%, you would be asked to pay back the loan at a rate of £40.58 per month for a period of 60 months starting in the April after you graduated. The total repayment would be £2429.54.

The likelihood is that you would need to borrow a little more in your second year, and possibly about the same in your third.

## If I'm doing a four- or five-year degree, and so borrow more, will I have longer to repay the debt?

Yes. While most students are expected to repay their loan within five years, those who borrow for five years will be given seven years to pay it off. You can, of course, repay your loan sooner if you wish.

## OK – £45 a month won't break me, but in reality it is going to cost a lot more?

Yes, it is likely to be at least three times that amount, and more than likely a lot more. It is impossible to give you any exact figures, as nobody knows what the inflation rate is going to be – or, in fact, how much the loan is likely to increase. But to give you some idea: if we take the example in the previous paragraph and multiply it by three to cover the three years, the amount borrowed would be £6255; your repayments would then be £121.74 a month. If that sounds scary then go back three questions – with earnings of £1370 a month, you should be able to afford it. But remember these are not accurate figures, and the loan has been increased by around 20% this year. However, it gives you an idea.

## THE NEW SYSTEM FOR 'NEW STUDENTS'

## What are the pay-back arrangements?

Once you have graduated and your income is at least £10,000 you will begin to pay off the loan. This is earlier than previous students, but the payments will be less and spread over a much longer time. So whether you have borrowed £1000 or £10,000 your weekly repayments will be the same if you are on the same salary and you will go on paying until the debt is paid off. There is no time limit on repaying the loan. Rates are worked out currently at 9% of income over £10,000.

So the scale looks something like this:

| Annual income | Monthly repayment(£) |
|---|---|
| up to £10,000 | £0 |
| £11,000 | £7 |
| £12,000 | £15 |
| £15,000 | £37 |
| £17,000 | £52 |
| £20,000 | £75 |

## How will I make the repayments?

Repayments will be collected through the Inland Revenue and will be deducted from your salary at source. Probably all you will know about it is an entry on your pay-slip.

## Will I have to pay back more than I borrow?

In real terms no. As with the current scheme for existing students, the interest rates on loans are linked to inflation. This is currently running at

2.6%. So that graduates repay no more in real terms, after inflation has been taken into account, than they borrowed.

## Is the new pay-back system better?

Many people think so, especially as it is to be collected by the Inland Revenue. It may take longer to pay off and the debt will probably be greater, but it will be is less painful as it will be deducted at source like income tax, so you probably won't notice it.

## How are my repayment calculations worked out?

| | | |
|---|---|---|
| Annual salary | £12000 | £18000 |
| Monthly income | £1000 | £1500 |
| Minus income disregarded (the first £10,000) | £833 | £833 |
| Income on which repayment due | £167 | £667 |
| Reypayment due per month @ 9% | £15 | £60 |
| Repayment of total income | 1.5% | 4% |

## Will all students graduate with a huge debt?

Yes, most students starting a course now will have to face up to the prospect of starting work with a debt to pay off, and this could be substantially more than the amount totted up under the Student Loans Scheme. Our research shows that 74.3% of students had overdrafts, some 67.7% had student loans, and a massive 82.5% expected to be in debt to either the bank or the Loans Company, or possibly both, by the end of their course – to the tune of £500 to over £8000 (£10,000–£12,000 were figures mentioned).

## Cash crisis note

• Check out Chapter 6 on budgeting – it might save you a few sleepless nights.

• Compare current bank overdraft rates for newly qualified graduates.

Estimated student debt

| | |
|---|---|
| 17% | No debt |
| 4% | less than £500 |
| 7% | £500–£1000 |
| 7% | £1000–£2000 |
| 13% | £2000–£3000 |
| 9% | £3000–£4000 |
| 11% | £4000–£5000 |
| 11% | £5000–£6000 |
| 15% | £6000–£7000 |
| 6% | over £8000 |

## Do the pay-back rules ever change?

They are reviewed every year to make sure graduates can, realistically, pay back what they owe.

## Will I be able to pay it all back?

As well as the possibility of graduating to a massive debt, most students graduate to a fairly substantial salary. Starting salaries for a 21-year-old graduate with a good second-class Honours degree in 1998 averaged £16000. If you are earning around £1333 a month, the repayments won't seem quite so grisly. But will you find a job? And are you going to be a 2:1 success story? At the time of writing this book, the employment market for graduates in the UK is fairly buoyant. Graduate vacancies for 1998 are expected to be 18.5% higher than in 1997, with more opportunities in the non-industrial organisations. But trends are difficult to read and figures misleading; 55% of organisations report an increase in graduate vacancies last year while one third reported a decrease. This was the finding of a survey carried out among employers by the Association of Graduate Recruiters. It's worth remembering that if you can't find work, the Student Loans Company will wait for repayment; the banks, however, may not be so sympathetic.

## I'm a graduate with a £5000 student loan to clear – is my new employer likely to pay it off?

When the loan scheme first came in, many employers thought they might need to offer the 'carrot' of paying off students' loans if they wanted to attract the best graduates. Whether the government was hoping that employers would step in and clear students' debts in this way was a question often discussed in the national press. In fact at least one major company did draw up contingency plans for a 'golden hello' scheme, and a number of companies we contacted said they were watching the market and their competitors very closely. Then the recession hit the UK hard, graduate openings were in short supply, and graduates were competing for jobs rather than employers competing for graduates. Employers put all ideas of 'loan pay-off schemes for students' on the back burner. However, market trends and influences change very rapidly. Good graduates are seen to be in short supply again and employers are quite genuinely concerned about the amount of debt students graduate with. So the 'golden hello' has quietly materialised. I say quietly, because few employers are keen to call it that. Among the schemes we heard of were:

- one-off payments with the first salary of £1000 –£2000
- £1,000 in first year of working, followed up by £500 in the second and third years
- 'see-you-again' deal whereby students who are made a job offer are promised a lump sum if they take up the job
- interest free loans to cover costs of starting a new job
- advances on salary.

One major company we contacted over sponsorship was actively considering whether the 'golden hello' was a more cost effective way of attracting the best graduates than sponsorship. It's certainly something to bear in mind when you're looking for employment, possibly in a few years' time.

## Is the Student Loans Scheme better than borrowing from the bank?

Most banks and building societies will give students overdraft facilities on special terms, usually including an interest free £400–£1500 overdraft facility which may be increased – so check with the bank. This is intended mainly to help you during that difficult period when your grant or loan hasn't yet arrived. The overdraft is wiped out as soon as the grant cheque is cashed. It is better to use the bank's 'interest free £1000' facility if your financial problems are temporary or you are certain you will be able to pay it back once you graduate. Banks also offer students longer-term loans at competitive rates which should be investigated.

But, in general, banks are not the best bet for long-term borrowing for students; the Student Loans Scheme is. (See details on pay-back arrangements in previous questions.)

It's worth remembering, however, that to get a loan you have to have a bank or building society account. If you already have an overdraft with your bank, as soon as the loan hits your account it will automatically be used to pay off the overdraft, so you might not actually find that you have more cash in hand to spend, though you'll certainly have more peace of mind.

## "600 Face Court Over Student Loan Debt"

Did you see the headlines in the newspapers a few years ago? Could that be you? The stories were high on drama but low on facts. Firstly, no student is ever forced to pay back a loan – you have to be in permanent employment and earning around £16,488 a year (1997–98 figures). A spokesman from the Department for Education and Employment suggested that the problem was *'not so much can't pay as won't pay'*.

But it's unlikely to be as simple as that in all cases. Perhaps in addition to a student loan, students have run up massive bank overdrafts which also have to be paid back. Perhaps, too, they took out a graduate loan to get themselves kitted up for work. Borrowing money isn't difficult, but borrow too much and paying it back is. The Loans Company said that their greatest problem was communication: *'People just don't tell us what they are earning or that they have fallen out of work, so we assume they can afford to pay.'* This of course won't happen with the new system of paying back loans because it is done automatically through the Inland Revenue.

## CAN I GET OUT OF REPAYING THE LOAN?

Yes:

- if you haven't paid it off by the age of 65
- if you never earn more than £10,000 (new scheme)
- if you die!

# WHAT ARE CAREER DEVELOPMENT LOANS?

They are designed for people on vocational courses of up to two years where fees aren't paid, and cover course fees (only 80% given if you are in full employment, 100% if not) plus other costs such as materials, books, childcare and living expenses. You can apply for £300 to £8000.

The scheme is funded by a number of high street banks and administered by the Department for Education and Employment, who will pay the interest on your loan during training and for up to one month afterwards. If the course you take lasts more than two years you should contact your local Training and Enterprise Council which may be willing to sponsor your career development loan for more.

**For a free booklet on Career Development Loans phone 0800 585 505.**

## Where can I get more information on student loans?

Call the Student Loans Scheme Help Line, free on 0800 40 50 10.
The Student Loans Company is based at 100 Bothwell Street, Glasgow G2 7JD.
Full information about the Student Loans Scheme is set out in a leaflet issued free and updated each year from:

*England:* Department for Education and Employment, 0800 731 9133; e-mail: info@dfee.gov.uk. Publications Centre, PO Box 505, Sudbury, Suffolk, CO10 6AU. Tel: 0845 6022260.

*Scotland:* Student Awards Agency for Scotland, Gyleview House, 3 Redheughs Rigg, South Gyle, Edinburgh EH12 9HH. Tel: 0131 244 5823; Fax: 0131 244 5887. For booklet: 0131 244 8075. Talking book version also available.

*Wales (Welsh speaking):* Welsh Office Education Department, FHE1 Division, 4th Floor, Cathays Park, Cardiff, CF1 3NQ. Tel: 01222 825831 Fax: 01222 825823.

*Northern Ireland:* Department of Education for Northern Ireland, Rathgael House, Balloo Road, Bangor, Co Down BT19 7PR. Tel: 01247 279279; Fax: 01247 279100.

*For Blind Students:* braille and cassette editions, RNIB, PO Box 173, Peterborough PE2 6WS. Tel: 01345 023 153.

There are many anomalies within the two schemes which we have not touched on here. The Student Loans Company issues its own leaflet, and do take advice from your college so that you know exactly what you are getting involved in.

## HELP FROM YOUR UNIVERSITY OR COLLEGE

There are a number of special funds you could tap if you get into real difficulties, for example **Access Funds, Hardship Funds** and the new **hardship loan**.

### What is the new hardship loan?

This is a further £250 loan which new students under the new system can apply for through their university if they get into real financial difficulty. The criteria for what is meant by 'financial hardship' hadn't been set when we published, so our advice is, if you are feeling the pinch, it's always worth a try.

### Will this additional loan just put me deeper in debt?

Yes, but it's probably better than starving and you will be able to pay it back through the new student loan repayment scheme which takes into account your earnings. If you're a potential high flier, it shouldn't be a problem.

### What are the Access Funds?

Access Funds are sums of money allocated by the government to educational institutions to help students who get into financial difficulties. There are three funds: one covers further education students, another undergraduates and a third postgraduates. The allocation to any institution is based largely on its number of students and local housing costs.

### Why were they started?

The Access Funds were originally first introduced to help students out when they were no longer entitled to claim Housing Benefit and Income

Support, and to ease the introduction of student loans. Now they are an integral part of the funding package for students.

In 1998 the amount allocated to the funds has been doubled to over £44m in England and Wales and £8.7m in Scotland to cope with increasing financial hardship among students. However, divided between the whole student population, that still isn't a vast amount.

## What can I get Access money for?

There are guidelines but no rules and regulations laid down as to how Access money should be distributed. These suggest that not more than £3000 should be given to one individual. Handouts are decided purely on the whim of individual institutions and what in fact they feel their students' financial problems are.

Access Funds have been used to help students with:

- rent
- childcare responsibilities
- setting up crèches
- adult dependants
- single parents
- travel expenses
- expenses if they are too old to qualify for a loan (over 50)
- bursaries
- the cost of fees
- course equipment

Some institutions allocate 80% towards rent relief; others as little as 40%. To qualify you must already have applied for a student loan. At Coventry University where rents are not a major problem, 75% of the money used to be allocated in fixed sums to students with childcare responsibilities. Today, however they have a different scheme. Students applying for Access money are asked to provide a financial plan for the year with some documentary evidence of their income and expenditure. This is then assessed by the Student Union Advice Centre and the shortfall for the year is calculated.

Asked why they have changed the system, John Brassington, who is in charge of Access allocation at Coventry said:

*'Childcare is one of the major factors which causes financial problems for students, but it's usually a mixture of other things as well; travel costs and the cost of equipment, especially for those on art and design courses. Rents*

*are not so much of a problem in this area but a mature student might be trying to maintain a home as well. So we look at the complete picture. The maximum we give is £3000. If the assessed shortfall is more than that we immediately chop it back to that figure, which sometimes is just not enough.'*

Coventry finds getting students to draw up a financial plan concentrates their minds and makes them think twice. 'Some students do try it on,' says John Brassington. 'We did have one student who said he was renting a room when in fact he was renting them out to other students. But

---

## Glasgow students in crisis

### Claire, English
I was having money problems but didn't want to ask my parents for help. A friend suggested that I approached my university adviser for advice. He suggested applying to the common bursaries fund. To do this you have to send in details of your weekly expenditure debts, income etc. My adviser also wrote a letter. Luckily my case was accepted and I got £200 – enough to sort out most of my problems'.

### Francis, History and Politics
I had been living in the flat for 18 months when I reached crisis point. I had no money, my overdraft was at its limit and the landlord wanted the two months rent I owed him. Then, surprisingly, he came up with the solution – he offered to pay ME £5 a day and let me off my debt on condition that I painted the communal hallway. Sounds like a great deal, I thought. But after six hours a day painting I'm not so sure.

### Pippa, Art
Imagine the scene: we had been living in the flat for seven months. It was home and we were comfortable. Then out of the blue a messenger arrives on the door step with a 24-hour eviction notice. Background: apparently the landlord had been pocketing our rent – which we had always paid in full and on time – instead of paying the mortgage. Final act: the mortgage company repossessed the house and we had to leave the next day. We had no protection because they had become the new landlords and our lease was redundant – it was most unsettling.

### Gordon, 2nd Year, Latin American Studies
When I came to university I had an electric guitar, an amp, a bass guitar, a stereo and a camera. In times of financial need these have all had temporary lodging in the pawn shop. Gradually this became less and less temporary so that now I no longer have a bass guitar, a camera or a stereo. The loss of the latter is no great hardship as I have already sold my records one by one to the second-hand record shop.

mostly the requests are genuine and the problems caused by hardship rather than financial mismanagement.'

## To whom should I apply for money from the Access Fund?

The university or college you attend or have applied to. Ask at the Student Support or Student Services office, or the student union.

## How do I set about getting Access money?

Every institution will have a different procedure and different criteria for measuring your needs. You will most probably have to fill in a form giving details of your financial situation. Most institutions will have somebody to help and advise you. They may even have a printed leaflet giving you details.

## When should I apply for Access funding?

As soon as possible. The Fund is limited to the amount that is allocated, so it is largely first come first served. We have heard of institutions that have allocated most of their funds by the end of November of the academic year.

## I'm a student from abroad – can I apply for Access money?

Sorry, but no. The Access Funds are restricted to 'home' students only, so overseas students will not be eligible.

## What are Hardship Funds?

Hardship Funds are administered by many institutions, and also by some student unions, to help students in real financial difficulty. They all vary depending on the institution, and will pay out money for a variety of reasons.

## What help will they give?

Priority is often given to students who are suffering financially because of unforeseen circumstances such as a death in the family or illness. Sometimes small amounts are given to tide you over or to pay a pressing bill, or to assist with childminding expenses. Increasingly, hardship payments are taking the form of an interest-free loan, which can be especially useful if your grant/loan cheque doesn't arrive on time.

Leeds University Union, for example, offers a range of financial assistance to students who find themselves in difficulty. There is a Fundraising Group which considers all applications. As the money mostly comes from external charitable trusts, their hands are tied to some extent because they are governed by each individual trust's guidelines and criteria. But they are successful, as the extracts from the following letters prove:

*'My English is not good enough to express my heartfelt thanks to you. When I first met you, I was in despair... I owe it to you that I can continue my study here.'* First degree student from abroad

*'I am grateful to you and your fundraising committee for your help. With this financial assistance, I can continue my PhD study and research work at this university.'* Postgrad in Electronic and Electrical Engineering Department

## BANKS, OVERDRAFTS, LOANS, FREEBIES

## Which bank? What's the carrot? What will they do for me?

Despite all the talk of students and their financial difficulties, and our research showing that most students are likely to be in debt by the time they qualify, banks are still falling over themselves in an effort to gain your custom. Nearly all offer students some kind of carrot to get them to open an account, and promise some kind of interest-free loan. Their reasoning isn't difficult to fathom. Banks are in the business of long-term investments. Students are the country's potential high earners. Statistics show that people are more likely to change their marriage partner than their bank. The strategy is: Get 'em young and you've got 'em for life.

So what's on offer?

Most banks keep their new student offer under wraps right until the very last minute – largely so that their competitors can't top it with a better inducement. This means the new offer is on the table from around June/July. Some banks have a closing date for their offers which could be as early as November, when the first grant cheques have been happily banked. The offer is generally open only to first-year students. Before giving you the benefit of their freebies, the bank of your choice will ask for some proof of your student status such as your LEA award letter or your first term's grant cheque.

To give you some idea of what you can expect, and to check the next round of offers, we looked at how students fared in 1997–98.

In terms of cash or cash in kind, Barclays is offering £25 cash on opening an account plus a further £25 with a Student Barclay card and £10 of cinema vouchers. Hard on their heels comes NatWest offering £35 cash on opening an account with a further £15 at student branches. With Lloyds you have a choice of £30 cash or £20 cash plus a National Express Coachcard worth £19, and with its sister bank the TSB it's £30 of Our Price vouchers. Other freebies included commission free travellers cheques. But, as Barclays pointed out: 'Our research shows what graduates want most is cash in hand.'

But should one be bribed into choosing a bank? Forward-thinking students may well decide that interest-free overdraft facilities carry more weight in making the choice than a paltry one-time cash offer. Here you would do well to look carefully at the small print before making a decision. Some banks offer more in the second and third years. But do you want that kind of temptation? Check our chart on the next page.

Looking even further ahead, what will your bank's attitude be to your overdraft once you qualify? How long will they give you to pay it off? What will the charges be then? How long does the interest-free loan last?

*'I went for the freebies – rather than the most sympathetic bank manager – bad move when debt loomed.'* Tanya, Glasgow

## Picking a bank: the student's choice

Most students in England and Wales choose one of the 'big four' banks; they all have branches on or near college campuses and students are well served. Last year Midland followed by NatWest attracted the most students then came Barclays and Lloyds. Over the border you'll find the two leading Scottish banks The Bank of Scotland and the Royal Bank of Scotland are generally neck and neck. As we go to print the Bank of Scotland is ahead, but the Royal Bank also has student customers in England.

**Check out:**

- ease of getting an overdraft
- rates of interest charged if overdraft goes beyond limit, and ease of extending it
- interest rates on graduate loans – some are much better than others
- what happens to your overdraft once you graduate
- proximity to university/lodgings of local branch
- reciprocal cash point facilities close to your institution – otherwise you could be charged for making withdrawals.

**NB Don't choose your bank just because it offers the best freebies.**

## What is a Student Adviser?

A Student Adviser is somebody within the campus branch of the bank, or the branch closest to your college, who has been earmarked to deal with student problems. They are usually fairly young, and they are always well versed in the financial problems students face. Certainly you will find them sympathetic, and full of good advice on how to solve your particular problems. But you won't find them a soft touch, as one Student Adviser pointed out: 'It's no good us handing out money like confetti, it just builds up greater problems for the student later on.'

## What is a low-cost graduate personal loan?

This can be a life-saver for the newly qualified graduate. It is a special personal loan scheme offered by some banks to graduates to help tide them over the first few months while they get settled into a job. Most banks offer anything up to £5000 (up to £10000 with Midland or NatWest), or in some banks 20% of your starting salary. A graduate loan can be individually negotiated. The loan could be used to pay for suitable clothes for work, a second-hand car, advance rent – whatever you need. But remember: nothing is for free, and if you already have a student loan and a substantial overdraft, this might be just too much

SO WHAT'S THE BEST BANKING BUY?

*Compare the current facilities offered by some of the major banks. The figures were current as of March 1998*
*NB Student packages are usually revised each summer, so check with the banks for the latest information*

|  | Bank of Scotland | Barclays | Clydesdale | Midland | NatWest | Royal Bank of Scotland | Lloyds | TSB |
|---|---|---|---|---|---|---|---|---|
| *Free banking:* | Yes, to within agreed overdraft. | Yes, (some charges: check small print). | Yes, if within credit or agreed overdraft. | Yes. | Yes. | Yes, provided you stay within limit of arranged overdraft. | Yes. | Yes. |
| *Interest on current account:* | Yes, when in credit. Currently 4.75 gross | Yes: 2% gross rate pa | Yes, paid monthly. | Yes: paid monthly. | Yes, paid monthly. | Yes, at the same rate as current account holder, paid quarterly. Cheque account: 4% gross interest. | Yes. | Yes, variable on credit balances, paid yearly. |
| *Free overdraft:* | Up to £700 in 1st year, £800 subsequent years. £1000 final year. | First year: £1100 2nd year: £1400 3rd year: £1600 4th year: £1700 5th year: £1800 | Up to £400. | Up to £750 in 1st year, £1000 in 2nd year, £1250 3rd year and £1500 in 4th plus years. | Up to £1000. | Up to £600 in first year, £800 in 2nd and intermediate years and £1200 in final year. | First year: £500 2nd year: £750 3rd year: £1000 4th year: £1250 5th plus year: £1500 | Up to £500 in 1st year, £600 in 2nd year, £700 in 3rd year and for one year after completion of studies. |
| *Student adviser:* | Yes | In nearest campus branch. | Yes, nearest campus branches. | Yes, in nearest students branches. Called student Financial Counsellor. | Yes in all branches on or near campus with special student banking teams at selected branches. | In some branches. | Yes in all student branches. | Nobody in particular. |
| *Low-cost graduate loan:* | No. | Yes, up to £5000, available up to 24 months after graduating. | Yes, up to £2000. | Yes, up to £10,000 at preferential rate over a maximum of 5 years. | Yes, up to £10,000 at preferential rate over 5 years or 5 years for loan of £5000 or under. | Yes; £1000–£5000 at reduced rate of interest with 4 years to pay back. Repayments can be deferred for 9 months. | Yes, up to £5000 with 60 months to pay it back. Optional 4 month repayment holiday. | See free overdraft, above, for one year after completion of studies. |

| | Bank of Scotland | Barclays | Clydesdale | Midland | NatWest | Royal Bank of Scotland | Lloyds | TSB |
|---|---|---|---|---|---|---|---|---|
| Professional study loan ie Medicine, Dentistry, Optometry, Veterinary Science, Legal | Up to £6000 in 1st year, and £8000 in 2nd year of study. | Professional Study Loan up to £10,000. Up to £20,000 for Law. | Up to £6000. | Up to £15,000 | Up to £15,000 with a Professional Trainee Loan Scheme. | Up to £10,000. (Medical, Dentistry, Optometry, Law only) | Up to £10,000 or ²/₃ salary. | |
| Career development loan | | Yes, up to £8000 | Yes, up to £8000 | | Yes, MBA loan. | Yes, up to £8000 | | |
| Cash point outlets | Bank of Scotland plus Royal Bank of Scotland, Lloyds, TSB, Barclays, Link. | Barclays plus Lloyds, Royal Bank of Scotland, Bank of Scotland. | Clydesdale plus Natwest, Midland, TSB, Link. | Midland plus NatWest, TSB, Clydesdale, Northern and Royal Bank of Scotland. | NatWest plus Midland, TSB, Clydesdale, Ulster, Northern and National Irish Banks, Link. | All major cash machines in GB. | Lloyds plus Barclays, Royal Bank of Scotland, Bank of Scotland and TSB. | TSB plus NatWest, Midland, Clydesdale, Lloyds, Bank of Scotland and six building societies. |
| Insurance | Preferential rates – cover up to £10,000 in total | Special deal negotiated for students. Cost depends on location and type of accommodation. | No special package. | Special student package. | Student Protector Policy, student travel insurance. | No special package. | Special student package. | No special package. |
| Freebies | Commission-free travellers cheques and foreign currency. 10% off travel insurance. | £25 cash on opening account and £25 with Student Barclay Card. £10 cinema vouchers. | Interest on student company loan paid on graduation. Standard Mastercard with £500 limit and fee-free from first year. Scottish Citylink travel pass at 30% discount. | £50 cash or 4-year Student Railcard. Free Mastercard/ Visa card. Automatic transfer to 3-year graduate service. | £35 cash with extra £15 at student banking service branches. Combined card account with no annual fee for 3 years. First Eurocheque Card fee waived. Commission-free travellers cheques and foreign currency (purchase only). | Free Eurocheque card. 3-in-1 Highline card or Cashline ATM. 24-hour telephone banking. Commission-free travellers cheques each year, discounts on travel, music, phone bills and insurance. | £30 cash, or £20 cash plus 3-year National Express Coachcard worth £19 and National Express discount vouchers. | £30 of Our Price vouchers for all new account holders. Free cheque account banking. Commission-free purchases of travellers cheques and currency with trust card control (£250 limit). |

---

## Cash crisis note

Never run up an overdraft without asking the bank first. They are much more sympathetic if you put them fully in the picture. And unless they know you are a student, you could find you miss out on the interest-free loan. Talk to your bank's Student Adviser – ideally *before* you hit a problem.

---

debt. The graduate loan should not be confused with the many other types of loans banks offer to postgraduates to assist with study. (See Chapter 6 page 175–6)

# HEALTH COSTS

## I'm sick and myopic, and I've got toothache – can I get free treatment?

As a student you don't actually qualify for any help, but as someone on a low income you could qualify for **free or reduced:**

- dental charges
- glasses
- eye tests
- prescriptions.

## Form HC . . .

. . . is the starting point, available from high street opticians, the DSS or post office. That will probably send you off on a trail leading to Form HC2, HC3, and HC5, and don't forget to ask the chemist for receipt form FP57 (EC57 in Scotland) to claim for free prescription charges and your dentist for receipt form FP64. If you are confused, and who isn't, then Leaflet HC11 will put you straight on the NHS, in general a HC12 on costs.

Try to get things going before treatment begins, or at least before you need to pay up. Otherwise, make sure you keep all bills and receipts, as evidence of costs. If after filling in HC1 you are told you are not entitled to any help and you think you are, give the DSS a ring; it could be that the computer is 'confused' as well – it has been known. It can be a long process, but it's often worth the effort.

# HIGHER EDUCATION AND THE DISABLED

## I'm disabled, and I want to go into higher education – can I get extra help?

Yes. There are a number of ways that you can get extra help, depending on your disability. If you follow up every lead offered here, it's going to take time, but the results could be well worthwhile.

## What's the starting point for somebody disabled?

First choose your course, then choose the university or college where you would like to study. Next check out the college facilities, and their ability to cope with your specific disability, by:

1. writing for details of facilities
2. visiting suitable institutions
3. having a 'special needs' interview with the institution.

Finally, fill in your UCAS application.

## When should I start getting organised?

Early in the summer term of your first A-level year, as you may have to revise your choice of institution several times.

## What financial help can I expect from my LEA?

Like most students on full-time higher education courses in this country, as a disabled student you would be eligible for the full financial support package for students described earlier in this chapter.

For courses that do not fall within the ambit of this system, discretionary grants are given, but this will depend very much on the generosity of your LEA.

## I am severely disabled – can I get a student loan?

Yes. As an undergraduate you would be eligible for a student loan regardless of probable earning capacity and therefore repayment ability once qualified. In fact, the regulations laid down when the Student

Loans Company was set up allow for the loans administrator to delay the start of repayment and/or allow a longer repayment period for people with disabilities and any disability financial entitlements you receive will be disregarded when calculating your repayment amounts. Phone the Loans Company Help Line free on 0800 40 50 10.

## Can I apply to the Access Fund?

Yes. Each institution decides on its own criteria for Access payments, so exact entitlements would depend on where you decide to study. You might even find being disabled gives you an entitlement. See Access Fund details on page 71. If you are a new student you can apply for the new hardship loan of £250.

## What extra money is available for disabled students?

There are three Disabled Students' Allowances:

1. Up to £10,000 per year for non-medical personal help – eg readers, lip-speakers, note-takers.
2. Up to £3955 per course for specialist equipment – eg computer, word processor, Braille printer, radio microphone, induction loop system.
3. Up to £1315 per year for general expenses – eg minor items such as tapes, Braille paper, extra use of telephone by the visually impaired, extra books or photocopying.

These allowances are no longer means-tested. Most authorities will require receipts or a quotation before you can claim the allowance.

## Can I get extra for travel?

The support package for students includes a set amount for transport costs – as a disabled student you can claim for extra travel expenses incurred if your disability means, for example, that you are unable to use public transport and must travel by taxi.

## What about Social Security benefits?

If you qualify for the Disability Premium, the Severe Disability Premium, are receiving the Disabled Student's Allowance because of deafness, or are already receiving Income Support, then as a disabled student you could be eligible for Income Support or Housing Benefit. The ifs and buts are never simply explained. The people to put you in the picture are your Social Security office or SKILL: The National Bureau for Students with Disabilities (see page 84).

## Can I get a Disability Allowance?

This allowance is available to you as a student. It provides funds on a weekly basis for those who need help with mobility – eg the cost of operating a wheelchair or the hire or purchase of a car. It also covers those who need care and assistance with any physical difficulties such as washing or eating, or continual supervision. The allowance will not affect your grant in any way.

## How else can I raise more money?

There is a wide range of trusts and charities which provide funds for the disabled. These are covered in Chapter 5: Other Sources to Tap.

---

## *Thrift tips*

*'Spend time in the library in winter as it's warm and saves on heating bills,'* 4th year Computer Science student, Dundee

*'Don't attempt to keep up with the social life of your rich friends,'* 1st year student Theology, Bristol

*'Take all the food you can eat at breakfast which is free and eat it for lunch,'* 1st year Medical student living in halls of residence at Dundee

*'Drink in the union bar, it's cheaper – better still, work there,'* 4th year Dentistry student, Dundee

*'Develop a love for economy baked beans,'* 3rd year Healing Arts and Psychology student, Derby

*'Take out your student loan and invest it,'* 3rd year, Nursing Studies student, London

## Who to contact for advice

- Students' Welfare Officer at your university or college, Students Union, Local Citizens Advice Bureau.

- SKILL: The National Bureau for Students with Disabilities, 336 Brixton Road, London SW9 7AA. Tel: 0171 978 9890. It runs a special information and advice service open 1.30–4.30 pm, and publishes a number of useful leaflets and books for the disabled. It will be moving in the near future, so check the address first (Telephone number will stay the same.).

- Welfare Rights Office or local Social Security Office; address should be in your local telephone directory.

- Disablement Income Group, Unit 5, Archway Business Centre, 19–23 Wedmore Street, London N19 4RZ. Tel: 0171 263 3981.

- Royal National Institute for the Blind, 224 Great Portland Street, London W1N 6AA. Tel: 0171 388 1266.

- Royal National Institute for Deaf People, 19–23 Featherstone Street, London EC1Y 8SL. Tel: 0171 296 8000 (voice); Minicom 0171 296 8001; Fax 0171 296 8199.

# 3
# PAYING YOUR WAY

## Work experience, working abroad, a year out, travel

There are many reasons why students work, either before or during their study course. In this chapter we investigate some of those reasons and give advice on what sort of work you can expect to find; how to go about getting it; whom to contact and what to read. There is also some helpful information on the travel scene, insurance and holidaying abroad, and anecdotes from students about their experiences.

## SEVEN REASONS WHY STUDENTS WORK

1. To make money (this page)
2. To get sponsorship (page 89)
3. Vacation work experience (page 89)
4. To get off the academic treadmill (page 91)
5. As part of their degree – industrial placement (page 94)
6. To travel abroad (page 98)
7. Altruism (page 102)

## Reason 1: To make money

Our recent survey among students showed that a clear majority work from sheer financial necessity, and the aim is to earn as much as possible:

81% worked during vacations.
21% worked at weekends during term time.
23% worked in the evenings during term time.

We didn't ask for their final degree grades.

While tutors frown and wonder what the effect working, especially during term time, will have on your studies, they are also realists and appreciate that you need money to survive at university, to eat, buy books and benefit from the university's activities, so students have to work. So many universities have set up their own Job Shops.

University Job Shops can be found in some 60–70 universities throughout the UK and more are opening all the time. They all seem to operate on their own individual system but have one thing in common – to find work for students during term time and the holidays. Pay is generally around £3–£4.50 an hour. And during term time, they advise students to work no more than 15 hours a week, although they can't insist.

Job Shops come under a variety of names. For example you have Joblink at Aberdeen, Clearing House at Edinburgh, Work Window at the University of London, TEMPUS at Sheffield and PRONTO at Sheffield Hallam.

---

## Fast facts on work

Why do students work?

- For money
- For experience
- To travel
- To fill in a gap year
- To gain skills

Where do they work?

- In shops
- In restaurants
- In pubs
- In camps in the USA
- On a kibbutz
- In teaching
- In offices

How much do they earn?

£3–£5 per hour on average.

## Close-up on three Job Shops

Cardiff University's Unistaff, one of the first Job Shops set up, has a 'drop in/phone in and see what we have available' system. Most of its jobs are within the university itself which means 'employers' are sensitive to student's study priorities. Pay is cash in hand, paid out weekly by Unistaff. They have over 1000 students registered and the weekly wage bill is around £5000.

Southampton, the latest Job Shop to open, had been going just a month when we talked to them and was basking in extensive publicity on local TV and radio. This had brought in a lot of response from employers. They also have a 'walk in and see what's on offer' system. On average 10–15 new jobs were coming in daily, but so were 60–80 students looking for work. Type of jobs included IT, admin support, clerical, secretarial, nursing care, driving, teaching. Asked if they would accept any kind of job Gillian Gregory, Job Shop Coordinator said, 'I do use my discretion on occasions. A request for "Tall leggy blonds, who look good in bikinis to work on a Turkish beach and entertain customers" went straight in the bin. We don't carry commission, only vacancies or pyramid selling. And generally don't accept anything less than £3.50 an hour.'

Tempwise, the Manchester University and UMIST Job Shop, started four months ago and is a pioneer in the use of information technology. Students register over the Web identifying what types of jobs they would like and when they would be available for work. When suitable jobs turn up they are e-mailed electronically. The student then contacts the employer direct. So far, they have advertised 500 positions to 2000 students. The electronic system works well because every student at Manchester University and UMIST has their own e-mail address and has access to computers.

Check out your university Job Shop as soon as you arrive. Jobs go very quickly. Most students want or need to take jobs during the long summer vacations. Your university Job Shop or that of a university closer to home, may be able to help you here.

An increasing number of students are taking a year out between A-levels and going to university. While the motivation for deferred entry is more likely to be the need to 'get off the academic treadmill' (see page 91), in retrospect many students feel that the money they managed to save during that gap year has put them on a sound financial footing and saved them from colossal anxiety in their first year.

If your aim is to save money, your best bet is to work as close to home as possible, where bed and board are likely to be at a very advantageous rate – if not free – and avoid travel costs.

Jobs aren't easy to come by, especially for six to nine months, and vacation jobs are even harder to find. But with a little enterprise, some initiative and plenty of pen and leg work, you should succeed.

- Try employers whose workforce includes women with young children, who might take time off during the school holidays – shops, supermarkets, restaurants.
- Try to find an employer with a recurring need, so that you can come back next year. McDonald's likes to have a team of students they can call on during the summer vacations.
- If you've got a skill – typing, shorthand, word-processing, driving, computer knowledge – it could be easier.

Students seeking evening or weekend work during term time will probably find it easier in a large city than in a small town. London students should fare better than most – which is just as well, since they are among the most financially stretched.

You are most likely to find work in: bars, restaurants or general catering, dispatch-riding (must have own wheels and a fearless mentality!), pizza delivery, office or domestic cleaning, childminding, market research, modelling, offices (temporary), hotels, and of course shops and supermarkets especially with the increase in late night and Sunday opening.

## Who to contact

- employment agencies
- job centres
- local employers on spec
- university Job Shop

## What to read

- Local newspaper job ads
- *Summer Jobs in Britain* (annually updated)
- *Teenager's Vacation Guide* (1991)

These two books are available from Vacation Work, 9 Park End Street, Oxford OX1 1HJ. Tel: 01865 241978

## Reason 2: To get sponsorship

Many companies like to test people out before they offer sponsorship. Often they will offer work experience during the summer vacation, or as an industrial placement either before starting your degree course or as part of a sandwich course. If they like you, they may well offer sponsorship for the whole or the rest of your degree course. There is no guarantee, of course, that the placement will bear fruit. The course director at your institution may well have a list of suitable companies interested in your particular discipline; otherwise it's a matter of writing round. Many companies don't advertise work experience because they are inundated with applications. Start with local employers. Living away from home, even if your employer helps with expenses, will eat into your earnings.

For full details of getting sponsorship, see the next chapter, Spotlight on Sponsorship, and check out the publications listed on page 133.

## Reason 3: Vacation work experience

Many students use vacations as a time to gain some work experience in an area that will help them with their degree, or with entrance into a career. Many organisations that are unable to offer sponsorship or industrial placement do offer vacation-work experience – banks, insurance companies, accountancy and law firms, for example.

You may also find openings into areas where sponsorship is impossible and industrial placements are difficult to find, such as personnel, marketing or publishing. If you are considering the media, advertising or journalism, you'll probably find it's MISSION IMPOSSIBLE. You could try some of the local radio stations, but it'll probably be unpaid work. However Aberystwyth reports:

*'We had four placements with a local newspaper and one with local radio, and a local PR company regularly takes students and graduates under the CPW scheme [see below]. They received payment and these placements have led to graduate jobs in all three areas of work in the last couple of years.'*

Work experience placements are not all one sided, the employer gets something out of it too. But getting one is incredibly competitive. 'Vacation placements are an excellent opportunity for students to learn first-hand what a particular career would involve,' says Simon Davis, partner with responsibility for graduate recruitment at international law firm Clifford Chance.

> *'Choosing the right career and the right employer are crucially important decisions which should be taken only after a student is as best informed as possible about the choices available. Spending two or three weeks with a prospective employer gives students a very good idea of what the work would involve and what kind of atmosphere they would be working in. A student should not, however, assume that taking part in a vacation scheme will be a short-cut to a job or that failing to take part in a vacation scheme with a particular firm will be a handicap. After all, there are a limited number of places on these schemes. Students who have been on our schemes are treated the same as everybody else in our interviews and assessment exercises'.*

Clifford Chance offers 80 vacation placements of two weeks at Easter or in the summer and currently pays £200 a week.

Big employers such as Procter & Gamble offer what they call summer internships to students on a worldwide scale. They too see it as a fair means of assessing students' ability and hope eventually to recruit most of their graduates through their internship scheme. Your university careers office should have details of these. Otherwise contact employers direct.

Small employers can be contacted direct or try STEP. This UK-wide scheme has been set up to encourage small and medium sized employers to take on students for an eight-week summer placement to carry out a special project which will be of benefit to both the employer and student. Opportunities are open to 2nd and 3rd year undergraduates of a degree discipline. During the eight weeks you would earn between £110 and £120 a week. This is called a 'training allowance' so you would not have to pay tax or national insurance. STEP stands for Shell Technology Enterprise Programme and is backed by Shell UK with funding coming from the DTI and DfEE. Last year 1539 placements were organised across the UK. For details contact your University Careers Advisory Service or look at the STEP Web page on www.shell-step.org.uk where you'll find an electronic application form.

In Wales they have the Cymru Proposer Wales (CPW) scheme, which is modelled on STEP and works alongside it. For details contact your university Careers Advisory Service.

If you are disabled then Workable is a good bet. Set up in 1990 to promote employment and training opportunities for disabled under-graduates and postgraduates, it seeks out work placements with major employers where students would undertake real work and hold down real responsibilities – a valuable asset on your CV. Under its auspices are LEGABLE for opportunities in the legal profession, INSURABLE for the insurance industry, MEDIABLE, ARTSABLE and Workable in the Civil Service. For details contact your university careers service, or student union, or WORKABLE direct. Contact Mike Moulds, Graduate Support Scheme Coordinator, The Innovation Centre, White-knights, Reading RG6 6BX. Tel: 0118 925 2912; Fax: 0118 986 7767; e-mail: mikemoulds-workable@e-mail.com; Web site: http://members.aol.com/workableuk/index.html

Oxford University Careers Service runs a special scheme called Vac Train, which seeks out employers willing to take on pre-final-year undergraduates for 6–12 weeks during the Easter and summer vacation. Currently it has 52 companies on its books, and last summer they placed 106 students. When first introduced Oxford believed the scheme was unique, but other institutions may well have similar schemes – it's worth checking.

## Who to contact

- Local employers
- Major employers
- Course directors
- College notice boards
- Your university careers advisers
- University Job Shops (see Reason 1)
- STEP
- Workable
- Vac Train
- Local employment agencies.

## Reason 4: To get off the academic treadmill

Taking a year out after A-levels – a 'gap year', as it is generally called – is becoming increasingly popular. After at least 13 solid years on the academic treadmill, many young people just feel that they need a chance to recharge their batteries. Most universities will accept deferred entry; many institutions – such as Oxford and Cambridge – actively encourage it. But don't assume that deferred entry is an automatic right. You must always ask, and if the course is popular, it may be refused.

Many young people use this time to gain a skill or experience in a specific organisation as well as making money, so that they have a ready-made job to walk into during vacations, once they have started their degree course. Others just seek fun and experience.

Here four students talk about their gap year with the army through the Short Service Limited Commission (SSLC) scheme. Most managed to save something during the year, but not a lot. They then went on to join the Officers Training Corps at university when they were paid for evening meetings and weekend exercise/training sessions at a rate of around £30 a day. Though helpful, it wasn't money that made them join the army scheme, but the excitement and adventure.

*'I learnt to ride, found my ski legs, visited four new countries – South Africa, Canada, Poland and Germany, but the most useful lesson for university was learning to work in a disciplined way, to get the most out of my time.'* Mark Burton joined the Royal Artillery. He is now studying Law at Cambridge.

*Having led an expedition to Sardinia for a fortnight, been on a skiing exercise in Bavaria, organised a three-week adventure training package in the German mountains which included trekking, climbing and canoeing, during my gap year, leading an OTC expedition 120 miles across Corsica and commanding a TA platoon on exercises in Germany while at university held no fears, just more excitement and adventure.*

*'At university you can always tell which people have had that extra life experience – they stand out. The money you get paid is obviously a help to students, but it's not the motivation. It's just an incredible experience.'* Emma Smith joined the Royal Signals for her gap year before going to Cambridge to take Medicine and train as a doctor.

*'I flew with the Red Arrows, joined an operational refuelling sortie over Iraq with the Jaguars, made 23 parachute jumps including free fall, went out on boat patrol, spent time with the UN on the green line in Cyprus which was just like stepping into a time warp. I came back from Cyprus to start university and thought can anything in the rest of my life be better?'* Taylor-Jane Fox took a gap year with the army, a degree in Business Studies at Bristol University and is now working for Carlsberg Tetley.

*'Having recently returned from a simulated war zone in Canada, charging through the prairie in a tank, firing live ammunition, washing from a water bag slung across the barrel of the gun and surviving on field ration packs and four hours sleep a night, coping with university is no problem.*

*'Getting on the scheme wasn't easy. There were command tasks like getting this barrel over the ubiquitous shark infested custard, discussions, general knowledge tests, logic questions, mental arithmetic and the impossibility of scaling a ten foot wall when you're only five-foot-three.*

*'The challenge and adventure is indescribable. Just imagine: you are closed down in the tank's cramped gun turret in 35°C heat. You get the order to load, you move back and there's an almighty bang. There is nothing like firing live ammunition – the adrenalin keeps pumping as the gun keeps firing. It was the nearest thing you can get to real war. Fantastic! It has to be the best gap year on offer'.*

Frank Simon joined the First Royal Tank Regiment, for his gap year. He is now studying History at Cambridge.

To find out about the Army's Short Service Limited Commission scheme, contact the Schools Liaison Officer through your School Careers Staff, or try the local Army recruitment office – the address will be in the phone book.

## Who to contact

- Banks, insurance companies, accountancy firms – many do offer work experience; always worth a try.

- Shops, supermarkets, chain stores – try to find an organisation with a number of local outlets, and one which offers a training scheme.

- Teaching – you don't actually need any training to take up a temporary position as assistant teacher or matron in a preparatory school. As an assistant matron you could find yourself darning socks and getting the kids up in the morning. As an assistant teacher you'd probably be involved in organising sport and out-of-school activities, coaching, supervising prep and classes when staff were away. The current rate starts at about £30pw rising to £150pw generally for graduates, with everything found – food, accommodation etc. Term ends in July, so you would then have two months' travelling time. Try Gabbitas Educational Consultants, Carrington House, 126–130 Regent Street London W1R 6EE. Tel: 0171 734 0161.

- Archaeological digs: it won't earn you a fortune – more likely nothing; subsistence pay is given only occasionally – but it can be fascinating work. See the Briefing Supplement included in every other issue of *British Archaeology*, published monthly by the Council for British Archaeology, Bowes Morrell House, 111 Walmgate, York YO1 2UA. Tel: 01904 671417. This gives full details of current digs. Subscription is £19 but the magazine should be available in public libraries. Students in full-time education can join the Council for British Archaeology for a special rate of £12 and then the magazine is included in the package. For full details of membership and details of digs in your area phone the Council. Alternatively contact the County Archaeologist for your district. The Council will have the address too. See also BTCV details under the section on voluntary work (page 102).

- THE YEAR IN INDUSTRY – see 'Name to know', page 95.

## What to read

- *Taking a Year Off*, published by Trotman & Co, 12 Hill Rise, Richmond TW10 6UA.

- *A Year Off . . . A Year On?* – Hobsons, Bateman Street, Cambridge CB2 1BR.

- *Jobs Before Cambridge*, issued by the Cambridge University Careers Service, Stuart House, Mill Lane, Cambridge, CB2 1YE or from colleges.

- *Jobs in the 'Gap' Year*, available only from the Independent Schools Careers Organisation, 12a–18a Princess Way, Camberley, Surrey GU15 3SP.

- *Working Holidays* – try grape-picking, yacht crewing, driving, tour-guiding, beekeeping – there's information on 99,000 jobs in 99 different countries. Available from the Central Bureau, Seymour Mews House, Seymour Mews, London W1H 9PE.

## Reason 5: As an industrial placement

The idea of the four-year sandwich course which included an industrial placement was never envisaged as a financial life-saver, but many students are finding that a year in industry, with a good salary, is helping them to clear their debts while they gain invaluable experience. But with more higher education institutions developing more sandwich courses, finding good industrial placements is becoming increasingly difficult. This is felt mostly where courses are fairly new and the institutions haven't yet built up a good rapport with industrial concerns.

In the beginning, industrial placements were largely for students on Engineering courses, but increasingly, Business Studies courses, Retail

---

## Name to know: The Year in Industry

If you are looking for paid experience in industry, The Year in Industry can help.

The organisation has extensive contacts with companies interested in taking on high-calibre A-level and BTEC/GNVQ students for a year's work before a degree course.

The scheme operates via 11 regional centres – in 1997/98 over 650 students were placed.

As well as 'on the job' training from their placement company, students receive additional training from The Year in Industry to develop their personal skills and business awareness. The Year in Industry can count towards accreditation by professional institutions.

The scheme sets a minimum salary for students (£130 a week in 1997/98). Most companies pay more. Some students are sponsored through university by their employing companies – many others are invited back for paid vacation work.

A loan video is available for schools/colleges.

**Who to contact:** students start applying in the September of their final A-level year. The earlier you get in the better. Interviews with companies are generally held the following January to May. Your school or college should have details of your local Year in Industry Director. If not, contact Brian L Tripp, National Director, The Year in Industry, University of Manchester, Simon Building, Oxford Road, Manchester M13 9PL. Phone/Fax: 0161 275 4396.

**Some comments from students**

*'The practical work I've done in the laboratory will be very useful when I go to university'* Mary Dawson

*'I'm sure it's the sort of experience I will find invaluable'* Michael Smith

*'I decided to do The Year in Industry because I wasn't sure what degree course to follow. I've really enjoyed myself'* Sarah Parry-Jones

*'I will be sponsored by National Grid through my university studies and have the opportunity to come back as a permanent employee of the company'* Giles Broxis

courses, Computer courses and many others include an industrial placement year.

The University of Wales, Aberystwyth has pioneered an initiative to give any student within the university, who is not already on a sandwich course, the opportunity to take an industrial year out. The scheme is called YES (Year in Employment Scheme), and currently over 70 students at Aberystwyth are saying YES to the opportunity. They come from a range of disciplines: Arts, Economics and Social Sciences, Information & Library Studies, Law and the Sciences. You can choose a placement that is relevant to your degree subject, such as accounting, marketing and scientific research – these are the most popular – or use the time to experience work in an area that is totally new to you, such as personnel management, journalism, or production management. You can even work abroad: YES students have recently worked in Europe, Australia, Africa, the Middle East, Mexico and the USA and with major employers such as Marks & Spencer where they follow the same training as graduates. Salaries vary from around £8000 (less or even nil if it's a charitable organisation) up to £20,000. The scheme has been going for over 20 years, and Aberystwyth is adamant – with some justification – that the skills learnt during the year out have enhanced both degree performance and employment prospects. The latest figures they print show that 75% of YES graduates were awarded a 2:1 or first-class degree, compared with 43% for the total graduating from Aberystwyth for that year. The percentage of YES graduates entering employment/ postgraduate study and research has been much higher than the overall UK figure for the past decade. Many students return with job offers, sponsorship, some even with contracts already sewn up. (See letter on page 98.)

A must for anyone thinking of taking a sandwich course, but not sure what's on offer, is the *Directory of Sandwich Courses* produced annually by the Association for Sandwich Education and Training (ASET for short). This lists sandwich courses being offered by universities and colleges of further and higher education in the UK – over 200 different courses in all. The directory lists courses per institution under various subject headings ('career areas'), along with addresses and names of placement tutors. A shorter version is available for university entrants. Both versions can be found on the Internet. A password will be needed for the full version but the shorter version is available to everyone. At the time of publishing the Web site number was not yet available. For details of this and hard copy of shorter version, contact: ASET Directory of Sandwich Courses, ASET Secretary, 3 Westbrook Court, Sharrow Vale

Road, Sheffield S11 8YZ. Tel: 0114 266 9999; Fax: 0114 268 3335; e-mail: ASET@ASET.DEMON.CO.UK.

## Who to ask

- If you are not a sponsored student, contact your department at your university. They will have a list of possible employers.

- Contact employers direct – don't forget that smaller companies which might offer just one placement often don't get deluged.

- Workable, which finds placements for disabled students – see Reason 3, vacation work experience page 89.

## *What to read*

- *Engineering Opportunities for Students and Graduates*, published by the Institution of Mechanical Engineers, available free from The Schools Liaison Service, IMechE Northgate Avenue, Bury St Edmunds, Suffolk IP32 6BN. Tel: 01284 763277; Fax: 01284 804006.

- *Sponsorship for Students*, available from Biblios PDS Ltd, Star Road, Partridge Green, West Sussex, RH13 8LD. Tel: 01403 710971.

## *Letter home*

Matthew Keating is a Final Year Environmental Biology student at the University of Wales, Aberystwyth. He decided to take advantage of the university's Year in Employment Scheme and worked as a marine and environmental science instructor in the USA.

Jason Wyatt is a Final Year Economics and Marketing student at the University of Wales, Aberystwyth – one of the many students who decided to take advantage of the university's Year in Employment Scheme.

---

Aberysthwyth, Dyfed
March

Dear All

Imagine working in a tropical paradise – blistering heat, cloudless skies, warm, crystal waters, and coral reefs teeming with irridescent fishes of every conceivable shape and size. How about sunburn, mosquitoes, swimming with sharks and stinging jellyfish? I experienced all of this and so much more during my fabulous year in employment, in the USA.

I worked as a marine and environmental science instructor for nearly a year at Seacamp Assoc Inc, an educational camp located on Big Pine Key, one of a string of islands extending from Mainland Florida into the Gulf of Mexico. The Keys are incredibly laid back, even by American standards – a stress-free place to live and work, where smart dress means a clean T-shirt! Believe it or not, I was employed to cruise a 27 foot boat out to the coral reefs, to teach marine science and snorkel with kids aged 8–18 . . . I would have done that for fun! Of course, I was responsible for the boat and the safety of the kids at all times. After a few months I was coordinating entire school visits and staff, and designing my own programmes too.

I had so many great experiences during the year, and made some wonderful friends. I even travelled across the States – and back – after my job, not to mention skydiving over the Great Lakes, hot air ballooning, and of course, scuba diving. Did I enjoy my year? Silly question!

Now I'm back in Aber, feeling motivated to work towards a good degree before I disappear off on my next adventure . . .

'Have a nice day'
Matt

---

# Reason 6: To travel abroad

What employer is going to give you three months off every nine months, or say 'Take a year off and see the world'? None. You will never, ever get holidays as long as this again. So if you have a yen to travel, make the most of your time and budget wisely.

When you start to investigate the student travel scene, you'll discover that there's plenty of help available. The path to the Continent, the kibbutz or Camp America is well worn. There is a plethora of publications and organisations, cheap travel firms, ticket concessions – even government advice – handed out to get you safely there and back. If that makes it all sound rather overplayed, pioneers can always be accommodated. Backpacking and interrailing are always journeys into the unknown. Things rarely turn out exactly as you had envisaged.

> Aberystwyth, Ceredigion
> Wales
> March
>
> Hi, Everyone!
>
> In mid-May an advert appeared for a job with Hewlett-Packard, in Germany under the YES scheme. I went for the interview, and six weeks later, I was on a flight to Stutgart for a 14-month stay. I had never lived abroad before, and I didn't speak a word of German.
>
> I arrived to find I was the youngest full-time employee in the Mechanical Design Division and one of the company's youngest employees worldwide. This all seemed a bit daunting, although my manager preferred the word 'challenge' – and challenge it certainly was.
>
> Within a few months the Mechanical Design Division was made into a subsidiary company called CoCreate and I found myself in front of a TV camera demonstrating my first completed HTML project, which had been chosen from the company launch. The launch was broadcast by satellite to CoCreate sites worldwide and watched by over 1000 employees and customers.
>
> With 35 days annual holiday and a good salary, I ex-plored France, Belgium, Luxembourg, Austria, Switzerland, Italy and of course Germany. The experience developed my personal skills, my marketing knowledge, taught me to speak German, and now, recharged I feel ready for my final year.
>
> Noch mal bitte!
> Jason

If it's a job you're interested in, try skiing instructor, courier, au pair, grape-picker, children's summer camp assistant, archaeological digger.

## Who to contact

- AIESEC, the International Exchange Programme finds work place-ments for suitable students and recently qualified graduates with companies throughout the world which are offering work experience for a vacation or longer placement (generally 6 weeks to 18 months). It operates in over 87 countries and is represented at 25 universities throughout the UK. Check with your institution to see if it has a branch, otherwise contact AIESEC United Kingdom, 29–31 Cowper Street, London EC2A 4AP. Tel: 0171 336 7939.

- BUNAC, to work in the USA, Canada, Jamaica, Ghana or Australia, start with BUNAC (British Universities North America Club). It organises various work programmes:

- BUNACAMP counsellors find students jobs working with children in summer camps, helping to look after them and arranging activities. Some experience of working with children is required.

- KAMP finds students jobs in the kitchen or maintenance/general areas of children's summer camps. No experience is required.

- Work America Programme enables students to take jobs anywhere in the USA. There are similar schemes covering Australia, Canada, Jamaica, Ghana, New Zealand and South Africa.

To meet the cash crisis facing many students, BUNAC has set up a financial help scheme for its Work America, Australia, Jamaica, South Africa etc programmes, which provides interest-free airfare loans, so you can borrow enough to get yourself there, and then pay it back gradually through your earnings. Those working or the BUNACAMP and KAMP programmes will find that their airfares are paid.

All enquiries: BUNAC, 16 Bowling Green Lane, London EC1R 0BD. Tel: 0171 251 3472; Fax: 0171 251 0215 or your university/college BUNAC CLUB.

- Try also Camp America, which recruits students to work in children's summer camps: Dept YO, 37a Queens Gate, London SW7 5HR. Tel: 0171 581 7373.

- Work on a kibbutz can be fun. You may have to pay for your own travel, but not for living expenses. Contact Kibbutz Representatives, 1a Accommodation Road, London NW11 8ED. Tel: 0181 458 9235; e-mail enquiries@kibbutz.org.uk or Project 67, 10 Hatton Garden, London EC1N 8AH. Tel: 0171 831 7626; e-mail: project67@aol.com

- Au pair/nanny: try adverts in *The Lady* magazine and *The Times*; also the *Au Pair and Nanny's Guide to Working Abroad*, from Vacation Work, 9 Park End Street, Oxford OX1 1HJ. Tel: 01865 241978.

- GAP Activity Projects Ltd arranges work to fill the gap year between A-levels and higher education. It has schemes in 35 countries including Australia, the Falklands, Germany, India, Israel, Mexico, Nepal, New Zealand, Fiji, Pakistan, Zambia, South America and the USA. Contact them at 44 Queen's Road, Reading, Berkshire RG1 4BB. Tel: 01189 594914. Office open 9–5 Monday to Friday.

- Courier – many travel companies will employ young people, especially those with languages, as couriers.

We have mentioned just a few of the opportunities available abroad to whet your appetite – there are many more. The list of books and directories available to help you make a considered decision is exhaustive. We have limited our reading list to those books which are free or probably within your price range, or those you are most likely to find in your local library.

## What to read

*Working Holidays*, published by the Central Bureau of Educational Visits and Exchanges – usually available in libraries, from any good bookshop, or the Bureau itself at Seymour Mews House, Seymour Mews, London W1H 9PE. Tel: 0171 486 5101.

- *Summer Jobs USA*, published by Vacation Work, 9 Park End Street, Oxford OX1 1HJ.

- *Summer Jobs Abroad*, published by Vacation Work (address above).

- *Live and Work in France ... in Spain and Portugal ... in Italy ... in Germany ... in Belgium and the Netherlands and Luxembourg* – a series of books giving details of temporary and permanent work in various countries. Prices vary. From Vacation Work.

- *Working Your Way Around the World* – offers authoritative advice on how to find work as you travel, with hundreds of first-hand accounts. Find out how to become a barmaid, kiwifruit packer, ski guide or jackaroo. From Vacation Work.

- *Working in Ski Resorts* – offers details on a variety of jobs from au pair to disc jockey and snow cleaner. From Vacation Work.

- *Teaching English Abroad* – guide to short- and long-term opportunities for both trained and untrained. Eastern Europe, Greece, Turkey, Japan – the choice is vast and varied. From Vacation Work.

- *Directory of Jobs & Careers Abroad*. From Vacation Work.

*'Students have the time and the opportunity to travel and experience the "ideal", of freedom. You won't get that chance again.'* Loughborough University student, back from Africa

## Reason 7: Altruism – voluntary work

Voluntary work abroad in Third World countries is not so easy to find as it once was, especially if you have no recognised skill, and many organisations seek people over 21. Some projects will pay maintenance costs, and sometimes give pocket money, but it is not unusual for volunteers to be asked to pay their own fares.

Conservation work is much easier to find, both in the UK and abroad. Once again, most of it is completely voluntary and unpaid. You might even be asked to contribute to food and accommodation. You could become involved in projects for the National Trust, the Royal Society for the Protection of Birds, on the restoration of cathedrals, working with disabled people and underprivileged children, painting, decorating – it's amazing what some students turn their hands to.

While the financial returns on both voluntary and conservation work are likely to be zero, in terms of your CV it could be of considerable value. Employers are impressed by altruistic and enterprising qualities needed for voluntary work.

### Who to contact

- National Trust – Working Holidays runs more than 400 Conservation Working Holidays a year throughout England, Wales and Northern Ireland for as little as £45 for a week's full board and lodging (from £22 for a weekend). A chance to stay in some of the most beautiful corners of the country. For full details write to Working Holidays, PO Box 84, Cirencester, Glos GL7 1ZP enclosing a large A4 size SAE with two second-class stamps, or phone for a brochure on 0891 517751. Calls will be charged at 50p per minute to cover costs.

- BTCV (British Trust for Conservation Volunteers) runs some 600 conservation holidays and a number of shorter, weekend breaks from about £40pw upwards. Pond maintenance, tree planting, step building, hedge laying, scrub clearance, drystone walling – the options are endless. Contact BTCV at 36 St Mary's Street, Wallingford, Oxon OX10 0EU. Tel: 01491 839766. For brochure Tel: 01491 824 602.

### What to read

- *The International Directory of Voluntary Work* – gives details of over 500 organisations which recruit all types of volunteers for projects in all parts of the world. It's the A–Z of voluntary work: from Vacation Work (see page 101 for the address).

*The Directory of Work & Study in Developing Countries* – an authoritative guide to employment, voluntary work and academic opportunities in the Third World. Ideal for those who want to experience life there as more than a tourist. Over 400 organisations in over 100 countries are listed. Short- and long-stay openings in engineering, disaster relief, agriculture, business, archaeology, construction, community work, medicine: from Vacation Work (see page 101).

## When should I apply for holiday work?

As soon as possible. There are literally thousands of students looking for work. Most of the directories offering vacation work are printed in January, but there's nothing to stop you making a move before then.

## Can't afford the books suggested? Look in your local library

Nearly all the books mentioned here should be found in the reference section of your local public library, and if they are not, your library might well order them for you. A group of you might think it worth while to buy some of the publications mentioned.

## Is it a good idea to work?

- If you are struggling to keep your head above water with your academic study then the advice has to be *no*, certainly during term time.
- If you feel that by taking a year off you might not be able to get back into the rhythm of studying again, again the answer has to be *no*.
- If lack of funds means you can't really afford to make full use of all the extracurricular opportunities your university or college offers, then the answer has to be *yes*.
- If you are skint, with an overdraft which is crippling you on interest, then you probably have *no option*.

- If you've had your fill of academic study and need a break, then work would be a *good idea*.
- If your CV lacks excitement then a demanding/unusual job/experience may be *essential* if you are to be snapped up by future employers.

These are the extremes. If you don't fall fully into any of these categories – and most students don't – then the best solution is probably to 'mix and match'. In other words, work to secure your financial situation and provide yourself with new experiences and the financial resources to enjoy even more. Six weeks humping boxes in a factory could in itself give you a valuable insight into life at shop-floor level, while tuning you up both physically and financially to spend a month exploring the Sudan.

## MAKING YOUR WORK EXPERIENCE WORK FOR YOU

At the beginning of the '90s employers were fighting for graduates. Then came the slump and companies cut back on their graduate intake. Some opted out of the milkround,* and employers attendance at recruitment fairs was down. A few stopped recruiting altogether.

---

### Thrift tips

*'It is much more economical to pay rent with bills included. It may look more expensive initially, but works out cheaper in the long run,'* 3rd year Performing Arts student, Derby.

*'Don't socialise, ie. drink, smoke, drugs. Just work hard and get a first!'* 4th year, Fine Arts student, Derby.

*'Man cannot live on boil in the bag alone. Learn to cook, it's cheaper and your stomach will thank you,'* 1st year Computer Science student, Southampton

*'Forget about eating, just drink pints,'* 2nd year HRM & Sport student, Cheltenham

*'Work in a fast-food take-away and eat your favourite junk food for free,'* 4th year English student, Cheltenham

---

* *Milkround: the traditional graduate-hunting season for companies which give presentations at universities in the hope of winning interest and applications from students.*

Today the pendulum is swinging back. Employers are recruiting again, many have increased their intake and in areas such as science/engineering and IT there is a shortage of suitable applicants.

But whatever the state of the employment market, the big career sort-out is incredibly competitive. All employers are seeking the best students, and there is an increasing number of graduates coming out of our universities. Last year for example, Barclays received approximately 5500 applications for some 150 vacancies. And most other major employers would have similar stories to tell. Obviously companies can interview only a small proportion of prospective applicants. So – how do they sort out the best? What are their criteria? And what do you need to have on your CV, in addition to a good degree, to make you stand out from the crowd and turn an application into an interview? We asked some major employers.

*'At Barclays, we use competency-based recruitment methods for our graduate schemes. This means that all stages of our recruitment process, starting with the application form, are designed to search for evidence of particular behaviours, or competencies, which we know are required for success 'on the job'. For example, our competencies include leadership potential, breadth of thinking and innovation. Positions of responsibility and influence at university or elsewhere are the ideal environments for you to develop a range of abilities and are therefore of vital importance in providing the evidence we look for.* Cathy Powles, on the Management Development Programme, currently working in Graduate Recruitment at Barclays plc.

*'Strong achievement, both socially and through personal skills, is what we are looking for. Evidence of energy with wider interests than just study. Travel, perhaps, work experience, or something you may have done at university which is outside the minimum published schedule. I also look for the black holes in an application form. Things should run in a chronological order. What you haven't mentioned may be of no interest to us, but if it's not there, it makes one wonder.'* Peter Forbes, Graduate Recruitment Manager, ICL

*'To avoid falling at the first hurdle, your application form must pinpoint your talents and accomplishments. A list in itself is not enough, what we look for is evidence. For example, trekking around Europe shows enterprise – that's a point in your favour, but it's what you learnt from the experience that interests us. Did you organise the trip? Plan the route? Deal with a crisis? Good communicators, team players, time management skills, energy*

*and enthusiasm are the qualities we are mainly looking for.'* Graduate Recruitment Manager, KPMG

*'We are looking for the next generation of senior managers and technical experts, the people who will drive our business forward, so the kind of qualities we are seeking – conceptual and analytical thought, strong personal skills, ability to influence and motivate others – can't all be demonstrated through a good academic record, important though it is. We want to know about other areas of achievement.'* Margaret Harris, Graduate Recruitment, ICI

## Fact check

84% of students we canvassed said they worked because they needed the money.

73% of employers we canvassed said they like the graduates they take on to have had previous work experience.

# THE STUDENT TRAVEL SCENE

It's all very well to whet your appetite for travel, but how are you going to manage to get to that exotic destination? This section looks briefly at the travel scene for students.

## As a student, can I get cheap travel abroad?

Yes, there are a number of travel organisations that operate special schemes for students. In fact you will find they are vying for the privilege to send you off on your travels, and often dropping the price in the process. If you decide to take the cheapest, make sure it is a reputable organisation, with ABTA (Association of British Travel Agents) membership. It's better to be safe than stranded.

## How do I go about getting cheap travel?

If you are already a student, your college Student Travel Office is the best place to start. There you'll find experts who will understand your particular needs and financial restraints, ready to give you advice. If you are taking a gap year, or your college has no travel office, then there are two big names in the student travel business:

CAMPUS TRAVEL: the biggest student travel agent in the UK, with over 45 travel shops throughout Britain, many of which are on campus or in YHA Adventure Shops. It also has an international network of branches in Belgium, France, Germany, Greece, Ireland, Portugal, Spain and the USA. It's been in the business for over 30 years and knows most of the wrinkles. Whether it's a working holiday you want, an adventure holiday, to see Africa, Europe, the Far East or the USA, Campus Travel will get you there.

Phil Griffiths of Campus Travel says:

*'We send students everywhere in the world – hiking across the Andes, searching for lost Inca cities in the Peruvian jungle, canoeing in South America, and everything in between. The student mind is very independent. Usually they'll say, "I want a flight to [say] Kathmandu; tell me: What can I do when I get there?" We accommodate that and understand. Most of our work is booking cheap flights and accommodation. They do the rest. They don't want to spend two weeks lying on the beach sunning themselves in the Med. They are looking for a more dramatic kind of excitement.'*

Contact your local Travel Shop or Campus Travel Head Office, 52 Grosvenor Gardens, London SW1W 0AG. Tel: 0171 730 3402/8111 for details of your nearest Travel Shop.

ON-CAMPUS CAMPUS TRAVEL SHOPS

Aberdeen University
Aston University, Birmingham
Bradford University
Cardiff University
Dundee University
Glasgow University
Liverpool John Moores University
Liverpool University
Manchester Metropolitan University
Manchester University
Newcastle University
Oxford Brookes University
Reading University
Sheffield Hallam University
UCLU

UMIST
Wolverhampton University

STA TRAVEL claims to be the largest organisation specialising in independent travel for young people. It has been in business for nearly 20 years and has a network of 200 offices spanning Asia, Australia, Europe, New Zealand and the USA – a life-saver if you are stranded. Of these, 35 are in the UK. They will help send you to just about anywhere in the world. Their International Help Desk means that wherever you are you can phone in for advice – provided that is, you are within reach of a phone. It is their policy to employ only young and well-travelled consultants in their offices – many of them are ex-students, so you should get sympathetic advice. The *STA Travel Guide*, their latest travel literature, is intended as a compendium to excite the real traveller, and with tips such as 'How to exist in the Amazon', 'What to pack for the Trans-Siberian Express', 'The dos and don'ts of hitch-hiking in Japan', plus travel anecdotes from their adventurous consultants. It does make for an interesting read.

Gillian Smith of STA Travel says:

*'About 60% of our business is done with students, and most of our staff are ex-students. The route seems to be: they use us as students, go off and travel and then come back and work for us. They then know the problems and pitfalls, have been to all corners of the globe on the cheap, and know how to advise and how to survive – that's important!'*

Contact your nearest STA Travel Branch or for information on Europe, Tel: 0171 361 6161; Rest of the World, Tel: 0171 361 6262. STA Travel Head Office, Priory House, 6 Wrights Lane, London W8 6TA. Tel: 0171 361 6100.

ON-CAMPUS STA TRAVEL OFFICES

Birmingham University
Cardiff University
City University
Coventry University
Durham University
University of Kent
University College London
Imperial College London
King's College London
London School of Economics

Queen Mary's & Westfield College
Loughborough University
Nottingham Trent University
Sheffield University
Strathclyde University
Warwick University
University of the West England, Bristol

## *Advice note*

Never pay full fare on bus, coach, train or plane. Take advantage of rail
and coach cards, bucket shops, classified ads, chartered flights, stand-by
fares, advance bookings, deals offered by student travel companies.

## What should I join before setting off?

There are six cards that all travel-hungry students should look into:

- **ISIC: £5**
  ISIC stands for the International Student Identity Card. It is available
  to any student who is studying for more than 15 hours a week. The
  card entitles you to discounts on student charter flights, some accommodation, and in some countries admission to art galleries,
  museums, cinemas and other places of cultural interest. It is recognised in more than 50 countries around the world. At the time of
  writing it costs £5, and comes with the ISIC Travel Handbook which
  gives you full details of the services offered, handy tips on successful
  travelling and places to visit in 81 countries around the world. The
  card is available from Council Travel, Tel: 0171 437 7767, or by post
  from ISIC Mail Order, NUS Services, Bleaklow House, Howard
  Town Mill, Mill Street, Glossop SK13 8HT.

- **Under–26 card: £7**
  Currently carried by 3 million young people, this card is designed to
  help young people explore the world. It comes with a free Discount
  Directory which lists all the special offers available such as low price
  air fares and cheap youth hosteling. As a member you will automatically receive a regular magazine keeping you up to date with exchange
  trips, projects, events and offers. The card also gives you access to the
  24-hour Travellers Help Line which will help with any difficulties
  you may have. It can be used in the UK as well, where cardholders can

get reductions at many budget hostels, leisure and cultural attractions, and in Europe where a further 200,000 discounts are available. Contact: National Youth Agency, 52 Grosvenor Gardens, Victoria, London SW1 WOAG. Tel: 0171 823 5363. Look out for special promotions on the card itself!

- **Go 25: £5**
  This international youth travel card gives holders who must be aged 25 or under access to reduced prices on transport, accommodation, restaurants, in shops and places of cultural interest, and not just while you are travelling. Similar in many ways to the under 26 card, but not so widespread, it has recently been taken over by the ISTC (International Students Travel Council) and its future development is under discussion. An informative travel handbook covering discounts and travel opportunities is available from Campus, STA or Council Travel (see page 111).

- **YHA: £5 (under 18) £10 (18+)**
  The Youth Hostel Association (who also provide a card) offer membership of the international YHA, which gives you access to over 5000 youth hostels across 64 countries. They probably wouldn't merit even a one-star rating, but they are cheap, safe – and there. Membership at the time of writing is £5 under 18 and £10 over 18 for UK residents. For non-UK residents there is an International Guest card which costs £10.20 – all available from: *England and Wales*, The Youth Hostel Association, Trevelyan House, 8 St Stephen's Hill, St Albans, Herts AL1 2DY. Tel: 01727 855215. Internet: http://www.yhaengland-wales.org.uk; e-mail: yhacustomerservices@compuserve.com. For *Scotland*, Tel: 01786 451181. For *Northern Ireland*, Tel: 01232 324733.

- **Young Person's Railcard: £18**
  This entitles all young people aged 16–25 to a third off most rail fares in the UK. Did you know that it also covers the London all zone One-Day Travel Card and discounts off network cards too? See leaflet for travel restrictions and useful discounts.

- **Student Coachcard: £8**
  This entitles all students aged 17 and over to a third off National Express, and Scottish Citylink fares; also some continental and Irish services – check with your local coach station or Victoria Coach Station, London or phone National Express Call Centre on 0990 808080.

## Cards-to-carry checklist

| | |
|---|---|
| Young Person's Railcard | £18 |
| Coachcard | £8 |
| ISIC | £5 |
| Under–26 card | £7 |
| Go 25 | £5 |
| YHA card | £5 (under 18) |
| | £10 (18+) |

# Who else could I consult?

The National Tourist Office or Board. Many countries have a national tourist office or board in this country. Most are based in London. London telephone directories can usually be found in the reference section of your local library.

**Council Travel**, a division of the Council on International Educational Exchange, is America's largest student and youth travel expert. With over 47 years' experience in budget travel, it has 50 offices worldwide including one in central London open six days a week. Council Travel offers a wide range of travel services in the UK, Europe and worldwide which include low-cost air fares with quality airlines, budget accommodation, car hire, air-rail-coach passes, Eurostar, travel insurance, ISIC cards, adventure tours and tailormade packages, travel gear and travel guides. For further information contact: Council Travel, 28A Poland Street, London W1V 3DB. Tel: 0171 287 3337 for Europe, and 0171 437 7767 for worldwide; Fax: 0171 287 9414.

## What to read

● The Rough Guide series covers almost every country and provides a useful insight into an area. Published by Harrap; cost varies according to the country. Try your local library.

# Interailing or Eurotrain: What are they? What's the difference? Which is best?

They are both discount train tickets designed to enable you to see as much of Europe as cheaply as possible.

**The Interail ticket** entitles you to one month's unlimited travel on the railways of Europe for just £279. It is available to UK citizens and those who have been resident here for six months. There are two tickets on offer under the scheme: the youth ticket for those under 26 which gives unlimited travel across 27 countries, and the over 26 ticket which offers travel limited largely to countries east of Germany. For full information contact major railway stations or Campus Travel or Council Travel (see page 107/111).

**The Eurotrain ticket** is for the more organised traveller. It lasts for two months and covers a route pre-arranged by you to suit your interests, sense of adventure and more importantly, budget. You can stop off anywhere along the route and for however long you want. Available to those under 26, costs vary depending on destination. For example: how about the Eastern Explorer covering London to Amsterdam, Berlin, Prague, through Hungary, Vienna, Zurich, Brussels and back to London for £256. To find out more contact your nearest Campus Travel shop or Council Travel (see page 107/111).

**Freedom Pass** gives you unlimited travel within the country of your choice. Available for 25 European countries plus Morocco for periods of 3, 5, and 10 days with special rates for the under 26. Cheapest place we found: Luxembourg £19 for three days up to £29 for ten; most expensive: Germany £109 for three days up to £159 for ten. The rest come in between. Try Council Travel for more details or Campus Travel.

## Advice note

Find out about any rail passes offered by individual European countries. Campus Travel should be able to help you out.

## As a student, do I need insurance?

Here the advice is: yes, you generally do need insurance when travelling abroad. Some work camps and voluntary agencies arrange insurance for those taking part in projects. Check this out, and check what it covers. There are certain reciprocal arrangements for medical treatment in some EU countries. Check out the details and get Department of Social Security leaflet SA 28/30.

# Travel insurance: How much will it cost? What should it cover?

For as little as £13 for six days' travel, the International Student Insurance Service (ISIS) will provide insurance cover for your baggage, ticket and health. Most student travel companies will sell ISIS. Take it out when you buy your ticket. The cost will vary depending on how far you are going and how much cover you want. Don't forget to read the small print.

|  | Campus Travel | |
| --- | --- | --- |
| *Price guide* | *No baggage* | *Baggage included* |
| 6 days cover | £9.00 | £13.00 |
| 14 days cover | £12.00 | £17.00 |
| 6 months in Europe | £85.00 | £99.00 |
| 6 months worldwide | £123.00 | £165.00 |
| Endsleigh | | |
| 6 months study abroad Europe (Endsleigh) | | £83.80 |
| 6 months study abroad worldwide | | £124.80 |
| 12 months study abroad Europe | | £153.70 |
| 12 months study abroad worldwide | | £243.30 |

For details contact Endsleigh Insurance Services Ltd, Endsleigh House, Ambrose Street, Cheltenham, Gloucestershire GL50 3NR. Tel: 01242 223300. They will then refer you to your nearest branch.

## Letters home

Susan Kielty is a final year History student at the University of Wales, Aberystwyth. Last year she took a year out through the Aberystwyth YES scheme (see page 96) and worked in the House of Commons.

Aberystwyth, Credigion
Wales
March 1998

Dear All

Politics has always intrigued me but I completely shocked myself when I ended up being offered a position in the House of Commons.

I worked within the research library. As you'd expect at times the work was routine and office-based, but more often I was involved in exciting and demanding projects such as going to an international conference, which involved meeting and socialising with foreign politicians. I was asked to write Parliamentary Research Papers, help recreate the Parliamentary database, alongside advising and helping MPs.

Having worked, lived and found my way around London, I am no longer afraid of stepping out into the 'real world' – in fact, I can hardly wait!

The year was not always easy, but an incredible experience. Having free access to Parliament was a privilege which offered a unique opportunity to be at the heart of government. News was happening around me.

I firmly believe the experience has helped me secure my first graduate job – my new employers were mightily impressed.

Best wishes and good luck for the future.
Susan

# 4
# SPOTLIGHT ON SPONSORSHIP

## A complete guide to getting sponsorship, and what to expect from it

Probably the best and most comprehensive way of raising extra finance to help you through higher education is sponsorship.

- What is sponsorship?
- How do you get it?
- What do you get?
- When do you get it?
- What do you have to give in return?

In this chapter we turn the spotlight on sponsorship, on the changes to the sponsorship market that have been taking place recently, and on some of the companies most likely to give it.

## WHAT IS SPONSORSHIP?

You've heard of big companies sponsoring events such as the London Marathon, the FA Cup and cricket. It means that they back the event with money. In the same way, companies sponsor students through college.

### What would sponsorship mean to me?

In financial terms, it would probably mean that you would be £30–£50 a week better off than your contemporaries at college, with guaranteed work during the summer which would bring in a further £1400 or more. But it's not all for free, and sponsorship is not just about money – it also includes work experience and training.

## Fast facts on sponsorship

| | |
|---|---|
| *Who gives it?* | Major companies |
| *When?* | For a full course<br>After 1st year of study<br>After industrial placement<br>For final study year |
| *To whom?* | Degree and HND students – all subjects, but largely Engineering |
| *Most sponsored subject* | Engineering – Mechanical, Electrical/Electronic |
| *Most generous sponsors* | Paper and Packaging |
| *Largest sponsor* | GEC |
| *What it's worth* | £700–£2000pa approximately |
| *Other plus points* | Work experience – industrial placement |
| *Will it secure a job?* | Helpful, but no guarantee |

## How do I get it?

1. You apply to a company which offers sponsorships. These are generally offered to students doing specific subjects.
2. You are offered sponsorship after a period of work experience.
3. Your university has contacts with employers.

## What subjects should I take if I want sponsorship?

ENGINEERING: Has to be top of the list by far in the quantity of opportunities. The figures have shown that one in every four Engineering students is sponsored. Rewards vary. If it's financial rewards you're after, then undoubtedly the packaging industry and GCHQ are among the front-runners, but it can't be stressed too much that experience for engineers is very often a vital component of their degree course, and this must be uppermost in your mind when you are looking for a sponsor. The greatest number of sponsorships are for students on Electrical and Electronic Engineering and Mechanical Engineering courses.

PHYSICS AND CHEMISTRY: Way behind engineering but with 18% of the sponsorship market it has the second highest sponsorship opportunities.

COMPUTER SCIENCE: Another well-represented area but demand is down. Of the 16 engineering firms we checked offering sponsorship, only 3 listed computer science.

BUSINESS STUDIES: Still doing well when it comes to recruitment, and although it has dropped back a little it is not doing too badly when it comes to sponsorship. Most firms sponsor only a few Business Studies students, and some not every year, but it's always worth a try. Many companies have tacked sponsorship for Business Studies students on to their existing sponsorship schemes for engineers. If you are trying to maximise on financial rewards, it could be worth looking at companies where the sponsorship scheme was started to attract people to an unpopular, unglamorous or very specialised industry. Companies particularly interested in Business Studies students include British Steel and APV Baker.

ENVIRONMENTAL STUDIES: A newcomer for sponsorship. Try your local council. Many are giving sponsorships now.

ECONOMICS, MATHS AND PHYSICS: There is a demand, but it's not that great. If you sift through company lists, you will find there is a need.

LANGUAGES: Even with Europe on every managing director's mind, there is no real demand for pure language students. You might, however, be fortunate with companies that are making it big in Europe and people like Travel Teach of Newcastle.

OTHER DISCIPLINES: You may be lucky – a few organisations, such as Barclays Bank and Arthur Andersen, will sponsor people on any degree course, but you have to be interested in finance.

## Who gives sponsorship?

Employers – largely to those studying for Engineering degrees, but a limited number of sponsorships are available for Arts and Science, Business Studies, Finance, Retail and Information Technology. The three Armed Forces also sponsor students.

## Sponsorship: disciplines sought by employers

| Broad subject category | percentage of employers |
| --- | --- |
| Business studies and related | 13.2% |
| Computer science/studies | 9.4% |
| Engineering and electronics | 45.2% |
| Physics and chemistry | 18.8% |
| Accepts any subject | 5.6% |
| Other subjects (eg law, polymer science, metallurgy) | 7.8% |

*Source:* IRS – National Industrial Relations Services, Eclipse Group Survey 1997

Sponsorship of students in universities and colleges has been going on for many years. It was originally started to attract more young people into engineering. Even today engineering is still the major area where sponsorship can be found. Latest figures (1997) show that the majority of student sponsorship is for Engineering students, though increasingly awards are given for only the final year.

## When could I get sponsorship?

- After A-levels or BTEC for a full degree or HND course.
- After a gap year spent with a company, between A-levels and higher education.
- After your first year of study.
- After a successful period of work experience or an industrial placement year.
- For your final year of study.

While a large number of sponsorships are still given to A-level students for their full three to four years of academic study, more and more companies are choosing to sponsor students later in their degree course, when a commitment to the subject has been established. During the recession many companies cut back on their sponsorship schemes, but in 1997 there was a small overall increase in sponsorship opportunities. In 1998 the overall number of sponsorships available is likely to increase by 27% and in the industrial sector by a staggering 46% (AGR survey).

Chris Stead, University Schools Liaison Officer of the IMECHE says:

*'The sponsorship market has changed over the last few years. Companies have certainly cut back on numbers and many offer only a final year sponsorship, but I think it has reached its trough. Many of the smaller organisations who only want one or two sponsorship students are now going straight to the universities of their choice and asking for who they want. This is largely to avoid having to deal with the thousands of applications which advertising in our publication would engender. There are some good sponsorships around which are well worth going after.'*

## HOW DOES SPONSORSHIP WORK?

There are no hard-and-fast rules – every company devises its own scheme. In principle it works like this:

As a sponsored student you would get training, work experience and financial help while at college to varying extents, depending on the company scheme. You might be asked to work for a whole year in the company either before or during your course; you might be expected to work only during the summer vacations.

In return, the sponsor gets the opportunity to develop close ties with 'a potentially good employee' and to influence your development. There is generally no commitment on either side to employment after the sponsorship. However, since the company has invested a considerable amount of money in you as a student, it is unlikely not to offer you a job.

## What to expect when applying

*'I sent out 50 letters for application forms and got back 10. I applied early in the September of my final A-level year, but not early enough. Some companies said they had already filled their sponsorship vacancies; others that they were not sponsoring that year. Competition is tough. According to friends it was a fairly average response.'* David Andrew, Durham, sponsored by ICI.

*'I was told you get more money and more experience if you get sponsorship, so I got the Engineering Opportunities sponsorship book and went through from A to Z. I wrote to over 100 companies, got back 60 application forms, was invited to five interviews and given one job. Perseverance is probably more essential than talent.'* Vanessa Leach, Bradford, sponsored by APV Baker Ltd.

# What would I get financially?

There are many types of sponsorship. Generally, the sponsorship will include a money grant given to the student while he or she is studying, and some form of paid work experience which is generally at the going rate for somebody of your age.

# Why do companies give sponsorships?

We canvassed some 150 employers. The reasons most often given were:

- access to high-quality students before they graduate with the hope of future employment
- opportunity to assess students over a longer period as potential employees
- chance to develop a student's skills and have an input into their training
- the grapevine effect: publicising our company among other students.

Here are some companies' comments on sponsorship:

*'Enables us to recruit high-calibre people and encourages more people to work in engineering.'* GEC Marconi

*'Creates greater understanding of chartered accountancy among under-graduates.'* Arthur Andersen

*'Provides a steady stream of young graduates who will hopefully go on to become the leaders of tomorrow.'* NatWest

*'Never underestimate the grapevine effect. If you treat a student well during sponsorship, others in that university come to hear about it. Of course, the same happens if you treat them badly.'* Digital

*'Opportunity to see trainees in work situations before graduation – it's like a four-year assessment.'* BPB Paper and Packaging Ltd

*'Input of fresh ideas into the company. Able to assess students as future employees.'* Avon Rubber plc

*'Gives students a chance to look at us and we to look at them, so if offered a job they will know the company – warts and all – and will stay a long time.'* British Nuclear Fuels

# APPLICATION POINTERS

Employers are – quite naturally – looking for the brightest and best students to sponsor; they want to have the pick of the potential high-fliers at an early stage. When many students first apply for sponsorship they have only their GCSE results and a headteacher's report to show what they are capable of. This can be tough on those who wake up academically after GCSE or who really excel only in their one chosen subject. But good employers are more aware than you might expect; selection is not on academic qualifications alone. Sponsors are looking for signs of those additional qualities needed to succeed in your chosen career: leadership potential, the ability to grasp ideas quickly and to work within a team. They want ambitious, innovative, get-up-and-go people who can think for themselves and get things done. So if your GCSE grades slipped a bit – or, as one student we interviewed put it, 'you look like Mr Average on paper' – think through what else you have been doing. Playing in the football or hockey team; helping out at the local club; hiking across Europe; getting a pop group together – it could help to redress the balance. Remember: the application form is the first weeding-out process, and you are up against stiff competition. This is no time for false modesty – you've got to sell yourself for all you're worth.

## The application form

*'The application forms were all different. ICI's was undoubtedly the hardest. Six pages of detailed questioning from academic achievements to your strengths and weaknesses. They were the only company to ask you to take an everyday household object and improve it in some way. I chose a can opener and suggested a different method of cutting. Would it work? It helped me win an interview.'* David Andrews, Durham University, sponsored by ICI

*'Having 60 application forms, I was quite an authority. Most of them were fairly straightforward, but some asked more trick questions like "Why do you want to join this company?" As 95% of the companies I had never heard of, it was fortunate they also sent a little booklet about the company and its sponsorship scheme. APV Baker was the last form I filled in – what's that about practice makes perfect?'* Vanessa Leach, Bradford, sponsored by APV Baker

Mike Willis, Training Officer at ICI, talks about selecting students from the company's point of view.

*'The first hurdle is the application form – ours is six pages long and full of searching questions. This is not admin in overdrive but intentional. Only the really committed will fill it in. Drop-out rate is around 50%, which is good. We then select the best, interviewing between 40 and 50 students a year. We look for leadership qualities, teamworking, analytical skills and creative ability. They then attend a 2–3 day selection process which is certainly very rigorous for young people of around seventeen and a half.'*

## THE INTERVIEW

Interviews vary enormously. Some companies give a full-scale assessment with psychometric testing, tricky questioning, and watching how you respond to certain situations. Others are much more laid-back and go for a straight interview. Whatever the process, if you are an A-level student it will probably be something quite new to you. Don't worry. The company will be fully aware of this and will not ask you to do something you are not capable of. Remember, too, that your competitors will be in much the same position.

Still, don't expect an easy time at an interview. Here's what a couple of sponsored students had to say ...

*'There were 16 of us at the assessment. It was to last three days. We arrived at a Hotel in Runcorn nervous and not knowing what was going to happen, which was best. I think if I had known how tough it would be, I wouldn't have come at all. ICI had received 2000 applications for sponsorship. They had selected some 50 people to attend three assessments and were intending to take on only nine.*

*'Their first words to us were "enjoy it" and I actually did. There were logic, psychological and personality tests and several interviews. We were all from different schools and parts of the country and in a way we were all in competition, but by the end of the first day a tremendous spirit of comradeship had developed.*

*'The best bit was a problem-solving exercise. It was a real problem the company faced, based on thermal cracking. I was selected to present our solution to a panel of ten engineers, something I had never done before. Acute nerves before, elation afterwards. A day later I phoned ICI and*

*heard those magic words – "YOU'VE GOT IT".'* David Andrews, Durham University, sponsored by ICI

*'When I went back for the second interview, that's when things started to get tough. There was a panel of three asking me about my A-level coursework – How do you do this? What do you do with that? I kept thinking, "Help, somebody, bail me out please" – and mercifully they did. Every time things got a bit sticky, a kindly engineer on the panel just changed the subject. When I came out the whole thing was a big blur.'* Vanessa Leach, Bradford, APV Baker

# WHAT ARE THE TERMS AND CONDITIONS?

## Do I need to do a year in industry?

Not every sponsor asks you to do a year in industry. Some just ask for vacation work. Some stipulate which year. Others leave the choice up to you. There is no right or wrong time to take a year out of academic study – just what is best for you, your sponsor, and the work you would be doing.

After A-levels, some students feel that they need a break. Certainly, if you work for a company for a year before you start your degree, you will gain an insight into the career choice you are making and whether the subject is for you. It could save you three or four years heartache – many employers feel this too. If you have any doubts about the subject you are taking, then this is possibly the most sensible route.

However, some students find that if they take a break from academic study it is very difficult – if not impossible – to go back to it. And some employers feel you need to gain some academic instruction before you can benefit from the training and work experience they give.

## The question of cash

Finally, if you take your year in industry at 20 you are going to earn substantially more than you would at 18. But if you take a year out at 18, the money you save will help to ease your finances once you start managing on student funding.

Another point to consider is that under the new funding arrangements students will still have to pay fees during a year out in industry. This will be cut to a maximum contribution of £500 and assessed against family income. If your industrial placement is taken as a gap year you won't have to pay this.

# What do I gain from being sponsored?

- Money to supplement your grant.

- Training – most sponsorships will involve some form of training.

- Work experience.

- Guaranteed employment for the summer in an area that will assist you with your studies.

- Chance of future employment – but no guarantee.

- Help with final-year project work.

- Opportunity to gain first-hand knowledge of the working environment where you might possibly start your career.

# What do I lose?

- Your holiday time is not your own.

- You would not be able to spend the whole summer abroad – going interailing for example.

- You have the chance to see only one industry/company during work experience.

- You make a career choice at 18 which may not be what you want at 21.

- You may be obliged to work for a company whether you want to or not, because of a payback clause.

- You may be asked to work in locations which are not very appealing and possibly a long way from home.

## *Comment*

Some sponsors do allow their sponsored students to gain experience in other companies during vacations, as they feel that it will help to broaden their mind and knowledge. But most are loath to do so, for obvious reasons.

## How much time do I have to spend with my sponsor?

Some sponsors demand you spend a year working with them either during your course or as a gap year before university. Others give you the choice. Most stipulate summer vacation work of six to eight weeks. Students often ask for more and may do Easter vacation work as well. Engineering firms are generally more demanding and the sponsorship is more likely to be geared to a sandwich course, so you could be looking at a full year in industry plus two summer vacation placements. One of the most flexible sponsorships we came across was BPB Paper and Packaging Ltd, who state in their sponsorship literature: 'Students are encouraged to undertake one year's work experience prior to university. This is *not* [their emphasis] compulsory.'

## How will my sponsor keep in touch with me?

Methods vary – some are good; others rather haphazard. It is important to find out just how your sponsor keeps in touch with you, especially if work experience is an important element of the sponsorship. Some companies, especially if they have an input into your course, will send a representative to your university to see you each term. Tesco, for example, has close contacts with the Retail Management Course at the University of Surrey.

### Planned vacation work

Other companies will hold special vacation-planning sessions. These are usually during the Easter vacation and can last anything up to a week. During these sessions you would plan with your sponsor how you want to spend your summer vacation time.

## Am I obliged to join my sponsor after graduating?

You are not expected to go around cap in hand. Sponsorship is a two-way contract: both sides can expect to gain something from it. Generally, you are not obliged to join your sponsoring company after graduating, but there are exceptions to this rule, and research for this book revealed that these exceptions are increasing. Companies are definitely taking a tougher stand, and seeking value for money from their sponsorships. Some companies, for example, will stop your sponsorship payment for the final year if you don't agree to join them after graduating. Because of this, many companies will make job offers before students start their final academic year. If you turn the offer down, then the sponsorship is immediately terminated. A few companies do demand reimbursement of their sponsorship money. You would be fully informed of these facts before you agree to a sponsorship. All the same, our advice to those seeking a sponsorship arrangement is:

- make sure any literature you are reading on sponsorship is up-to-date – school and college careers libraries are notorious for displaying last year's information
- look at your contract in detail, and above all, check all the small print
- question your sponsor; they will respect you for that.

## Comment

The Armed Forces are slightly different from other employers; they have always included service as part of their sponsorship schemes.

## Reasons given by employers for cutting back sponsorship

- The amount that is being invested in students
- Poor retention rates
- The pull of more glamorous and better-paid career areas such as finance
- Staff reductions
- Increase in number of graduates.

## Statistical note

Latest figures show that around 50–60% of students join their sponsoring employer. However, some companies are reporting a 100% acceptance of job offers to sponsored students. As Mike Willis of ICI points out: 'Not so many good engineers are being lured by the bright lights and big money gains in the City.'

## Can my sponsor terminate my sponsorship?

Sponsorship is a legal contract. Look at the terms carefully. Most agreements will have a clause which allows the employer to withdraw if your academic performance is unsatisfactory. There may be other clauses you should watch out for.

## What exactly is meant by academic performance?

If you fail the odd exam, you're probably all right, but if your end-of-year results are so bad that you have to repeat the year, you may find that your sponsor is no longer interested.

## What is a sponsorship worth to me?

Looking at it purely in cash terms, bursaries given during academic study vary from about £500 to £2000 a year. More is an exception. There are people who give higher rates, such as the Armed Forces, but these organisations have a rather different kind of arrangement. We tried to find a meaningful average: £1300pa was about right.

Add to this the salary you could expect to earn during a year in industry – again, this varies. Salaries are generally age-related, so it depends which year you take out. A third-year student would earn considerably more than a pre-degree student. Salaries we checked out fell between £8000 and £16,000.

You would also be paid for summer vacation work. This again is based on an age-related salary, so you should earn more in your second vacation period than in your first. Some students work the full summer vacation. Companies generally stipulate a minimum of six to eight weeks. Average pay is £825 a month (IRS survey) which over an eight-week period would be worth about £1650.

From the employer's point of view the costs don't stop there. Generally a sponsorship includes training, which may well mean several weeks at their training centre. Some companies provide a personal tutor for students. There are also courses and meetings to arrange work experience. All this takes time, and time costs money. Every time somebody stops to tell you how to do something, it's worktime lost to the employer.

# How do I choose a sponsor?

Asked what was the best way to choose a sponsor, one student said: 'If he covers your subject, be practical – go for the cash.' Certainly cash is something to be borne in mind, but there are many factors to take into consideration even when you're looking at the money:

1. Compare salaries and bursaries: the plus of one might rule out the minus of another. Ford, for example, offer a fairly low bursary starting at around £600, but their monthly salary ranges from £1012 in the first year to £1519 in the fourth.
2. Training and work experience: this must be the real deciding factor. How you spend your time in industry could make all the difference to your degree results, and so to your future career.

- Check out the training schemes. Engineers who will eventually be seeking chartered status should ensure that the training they get is recognised by the appropriate institution.

- Check what you will be doing during working periods: whether you are just an extra pair of hands, or on a well-organised programme of development. Companies with sponsorship experience, and therefore well tried and tested sponsorship schemes, may be the best bet.

- Talk to other students on the scheme; what looks good on paper may not work out so well in practice.

- Find out what projects have been undertaken by sponsored students in the past.

- Check how many sponsored students join the company as graduates.

3. Ask yourself: is this the sort of company where I would want to make my career? A sponsorship puts you in a good position for eventual employment.
4. Geographical location: if you are a Northerner born and bred, think twice before joining a company that operates only in the South, or vice versa. Your industrial placements will be spent on your sponsor's premises, and that might not be in your home town. Perhaps that could be fun for a year, but is it where you would want to work after qualifying?
5. Accommodation and travel: if you have to stay away from home during work periods, will your sponsor help with accommodation costs and travel? If they won't, that could eat into your salary.

6. Work abroad: occasionally some companies – Ford, Arthur Andersen, ICI for example – offer work experience abroad for summer vacation placements to a few sponsored students.
7. Outsider or employee: some companies treat their sponsored students as employees, giving them many of the same benefits – eg 22½% off the price of a car at Ford.
8. Check for a payback clause in case you don't join your sponsor when you graduate. Check also if sponsored students are dropped from the scheme if they don't agree to join the company in their final year.

## Comment: That year's industrial training – an exciting adventure or a time of loneliness?

At school, and then at college, you are surrounded by people of your own age, people who want to do the same things as you. Friends are easily found. This may not be the case once you are at work. It is always exciting to go to new places and have new experiences, but if your work placement means being away from home, it's worth finding out where you will be staying, who you will be with, how often you will get home and what there is to do in the evenings. Most companies are well aware of the problems of slotting young people into a new environment and have contingency plans, but not all.

# HOW DO I GO ABOUT IT

## When should I apply for sponsorship?

**Full degree course sponsorship:** Some companies offer sponsorship for your full degree course. Applications for these schemes should be made early in your final school year, and at least by the time you send in your UCAS form.

**Second-year degree course sponsorship:** Some sponsors like to see commitment to their course among students before offering sponsorship. Applications should be made early in your first year at university. Ask your department head for likely sponsors.

**Final-year degree course sponsorship:** Increasingly, employers are offering sponsorship to students for just the final year of their degree course. Often this will be offered after a successful industrial placement year, or a summer vacation period. Employers offering sponsorship at this stage will expect students to agree to join them after graduation.

## What's the competition for sponsorship?

Phenomenal. All sponsors say that applications outstrip sponsorships available, and it is getting worse – so get in early. The earlier you apply, the better. Applications for full course sponsorship should have been made by the time you send in your UCAS form.

## How many companies should I apply to?

Students we asked thought around ten applications, but we did hear of people applying to over 20 companies.

## What is a sandwich course?

A sandwich course is primarily an academic training which includes within it an element of practical training in industry. The sandwich can be made up in a variety of ways – described as either thick or thin sandwiches.

## A thick or a thin sandwich – which is best?

The thick sandwich is generally four years with one year – generally the third – spent in industry. But it can be a five-year course with two years on a degree course, one year in industry, a final year back on the degree course and a further year in industry. Yet another five-year option is the 1.3.1 package, which offers one year in industry, three on a degree course, and the final year back in industry. This is rather less integrated into your degree course. The thin sandwich will most probably be a four-year course with alternate six-month periods spent in industry and education. Often a pre-degree industrial year is taken. Courses at Brunel are organised on this basis.

Which is best? That depends on how you like to work. Some people like the idea of their academic study being well integrated into their practical work. Others find interruptions of practical work disrupting.

# What is a sponsor looking for?

A straw poll amongst sponsors suggested that sponsors favour students with:

- good A-level grades
- maturity
- potential
- ambition
- evident team skills
- a sense of humour
- a hard-working attitude
- the ability to get a good second-class degree
- interest in their degree topic
- ability to assimilate information and learn quickly.

# What if I'm turned down for sponsorship?

Don't get disheartened if you get turned down by them all. Remember: there are an increasing number of students chasing a limited number of sponsorships, and the picture is changing all the time. You can always try again. Check out the section in Chapter 3 on getting work experience.

# Which comes first – UCAS or sponsorship?

They both come at once, which makes for complications. However, they are aware of this, so a system has been worked out.

First you should discover whether a sponsor you are interested in requires you to gain a place on a particular course – if so, you should name that course on your UCAS form.

However, it could happen that an employer you had not originally been very interested in offers you a sponsorship with the proviso that you gain a place on a course not named in your selection on your application form. While UCAS do not generally allow students to make alterations to their original application, in the case of sponsorship they usually relax this rule.

### Deferred entry?
Another complication is whether you want deferred entry or not. If you get sponsorship, your sponsor may require you to do a pre-degree year in industry, but at application time you may not know this. If in doubt,

apply for the current year. It is always easier to ask a university to defer your entry rather than bring it forward. On some courses, especially popular courses such as Law, deferment may be more difficult to arrange.

## People who can help you to get sponsorship

If you haven't been able to arrange sponsorship or work experience for yourself, The Year in Industry might be able to help you. Full details of this organisation, and the address to write to, are given in Chapter 3 (page 95).

## Am I guaranteed a job at the end of a sponsorship?

No. Employers are under no obligation to offer you a job and are unlikely to promise you one when they agree to sponsor you, so don't bank on it. Their intention in sponsoring you is eventual employment, but there are many reasons why things don't quite work out as planned – for example:

- there is a recession
- the company's plans change and the area of work you are involved in disappears
- you do not come up to expectations
- your own career ideas have changed.

Employers invest a great deal of time, energy and money in sponsoring a student, and they are loath to let that investment go to waste.

## Will my university find me sponsorship?

If you are accepted on to a course either conditionally or unconditionally, it is always a good idea to ask the course director if they know of any sponsoring companies. Often they will have a list. Some students will find that they are automatically offered sponsors to apply to, and on some courses where employers actually sponsor the course, sponsors are involved in the selection procedure. College prospectuses may give you some guidance. A number of universities advertise sponsored courses in *Engineering Opportunities for Students and Graduates* – for details see What to read on page 133.

Warwick University runs a special Student Sponsorship Office which has a large database of information on sponsorship schemes, covering a wide range of subject areas. While the service is primarily for Warwick students and those who receive a conditional offer from the university, they do provide a special 'advice' pack they send out to other students who apply. For further information, contact: The Student Sponsorship Office, The University of Warwick, Coventry CV4 7AL. Tel: 01203 524239; Fax: 01203 524 220. UMIST also has a similar scheme.

David Cox, Student Sponsorship Officer at Warwick says: 'Last year we had a large number of enquiries from pre-university students. Sponsorship opportunities look even more attractive in these days of student loans and diminishing grants.'

## Who to contact

- The Year in Industry – 'Name to Know' (see page 95).

- Local employers that interest you – many employers prefer to sponsor local students. Don't forget the smaller companies. Some may never have thought of offering work experience before, so it can be a matter of making yourself sound a good bet.

- Your course director.

- Your university or college may well have a list of sponsors who are interested in sponsoring students on your particular course. Some universities advertise in the books below.

## *What to read*

- *Sponsorship for Students*: this lists a large number of companies, industrial organizations and funding bodies that can provide sponsorships. It is published annually by Hobsons Publishing plc. in conjunction with CRAC, and is available from BIBLIOS PDS Ltd, Star Road, Partridge Green, West Sussex RH13 8LD. Tel: 01403 710 971.

- *Everything You Wanted to Know about Sponsorship*, regularly updated and published by Amoeba Publications, Lakeside Manor Farm, Crowland Road, Eye Green, Cambridgeshire PE6 7TT. Tel: 01733 223113.

- *Engineering Opportunities for Students and Graduates*, published by the Institution of Mechanical Engineers on behalf of the engineering profession. It lists around 40 sponsors and universities with sponsored courses and is available *free* from The Schools Liaison Service IMechE, Northgate Avenue, Bury St Edmunds, Suffolk IP32 6BN. Tel: 01284 763277; Fax: 01284 804006.

## Not all sponsors advertise

If you look down the list of sponsors in most sponsorship books, you will be surprised how many large companies appear not to offer sponsorship or work experience, yet do. Many companies just don't have to bother to advertise – the requests flood in anyway. They are so inundated with applicants that they have more than they can handle. To reduce applications and the need to advertise, other companies will have special relationships with selected schools or universities. So just because a company doesn't advertise sponsorship, that shouldn't stop you from asking. A well-phrased letter may do you some good, and it can never do you any harm. After all, any company should be pleased that you are interested in them. You might even find that your application jogs them into doing something. That's what happened to David Stephens when he wrote to Arthur Andersen.

> *'After my A-levels I wanted to take a break from academic study; I also wanted to travel. But to do that, I needed some money. I wrote to a number of accountancy firms. Arthur Andersen offered me the best deal.*
>
> *'I would join the new intake of graduates, do the same training, gain the same auditing experience, earn the same money, but work for only six months. I wanted to cram as much as I could into that gap year. Arthur Andersen understood.*
>
> *'They had no sponsoring scheme at the time, but I wanted to continue the relationship, so suggested they considered sponsoring me through university. They hummed and hawed and then agreed.'*

Arthur Andersen confirmed that their scheme had evolved rather than been a conscious decision to fill a need. Ten years ago, four A-level students wrote to them asking for work experience during a pre-university year; David was one of them. They proved to be first-class students and the firm soon realised this was an excellent way of attracting high-fliers at an early stage. The following year they took on another five students and the next year extended the scheme to 35. By the following year they were looking for 50 – and so it snowballed.

## Don't forget the smaller companies

If you're thinking in terms of your CV, it must be admitted that a well-known name will carry more weight than a smaller company. A big company that is used to taking on sponsored students may be better organised and give you better experience and training, but this is not necessarily so. Less well-known companies, and newcomers to sponsorship, don't attract the same number of applicants as the big names, so there's less competition.

## Will sponsorship be good for my CV?

Yes – but with reservations; 73% of the companies we asked said sponsorship was a plus point. The others felt that it made little difference. A Careers Adviser at Bath University, said that while sponsorship on your CV shows that you have been 'selected', it was the work experience that would be seen as the important element on a CV.

Of course employers will probably ask why you didn't join the company that sponsored you, so you will need to have a well-phrased answer. Most employers realise that a decision made at the age of 18 may not look so right when you are 22. It's always worth remembering that your would-be new employer may write to your sponsor for a reference, so it's important to leave your sponsoring company on good terms.

## Is it best to apply to local companies?

It is always best to apply to a company that interests you. Nevertheless, some companies do prefer to take on local people. From their point of view, there is no accommodation problem when it comes to work experience, and statistics show that many students want to return to their own home town to work when they complete their studies. So the company is more likely to keep the sponsored student as an employee.

## Is sponsorship always the best idea?

Generally, sponsoring companies will want you to undertake all your industrial placement and work experience with them. While this often means that your work periods are better planned, it can also mean that the experience you gain is restricted to a specific area or work environment, and only one company. This could limit your view and outlook.

As you can see, there are pluses and minuses on both sides. A company that is prepared to move you around its different departments and sites has a great deal to offer.

## Are graduates who have been sponsored paid more?

Often. A recent survey published by the Association of Graduate Recruiters showed that sponsored recruits and those who have undertaken relevant work experience were gradually being paid starting salaries that were some £750 higher than graduates with no work experience.

## The Armed Services

The three armed services offer very generous sponsorships. But their Cadetship and Bursary schemes are not open-ended. There is a service commitment involved and those taking them up should think very carefully about what they are getting involved in. Full details are available from:

- Army Officer Entry, Department 2763, Freepost 4335, Bristol BS1 3YX. Tel: 0345 300111.
- Royal Air Force, Officer Careers, Freepost 4335, Bristol BS1 3YX.
- The Royal Navy and Royal Marines Careers Service, Dept BH94432, FREEPOST 4335, Bristol BS1 3YX. Tel: 0345 300123.

## Can I get sponsorship once I've started my degree?

Yes. As we said in answer to 'When should I apply for sponsorship?', more and more companies are giving sponsorship just for the final year or from the second year of a course. These sponsorships often develop from a successful period of work experience during the summer vacations, or through an industrial placement during a sandwich course. Typical examples are British Aerospace, GEC, and Barclays.

## Advice note

Been unlucky in securing sponsorship? Try the backdoor entry. When you're looking for a summer vacation job, seek out companies that you feel could be interested in sponsoring your particular skills. You may be lucky, there's no harm in asking.

## Should sponsorship determine which course choose?

In theory no. First you should decide on the course that best suits you. You're going to spend at least three solid years and possibly more studying, so make sure you're going to enjoy it, otherwise the results could be at best disappointing and at worst disastrous. It's no good studying Paper Science because some of the most lucrative sponsorships are given for this area, if you're really interested in History or Geophysics. However, if you are particularly interested in gaining work experience in a certain company, or there are several courses you are interested in, and by opting for one it could lead to sponsorship, then obviously sponsorship should influence your choice.

## I'm a sponsored student, but find I don't like the course I'm studying. What can I do?

This happens. You choose a course in something that perhaps you have never studied before, and after a term or so you discover that you and the subject just don't get along together. A sponsorship is not a life sentence, neither is a degree course. Talk first to your college tutor. It may be just one aspect of the course you don't like. Then talk to your sponsor. You will probably be able to change your degree course, but it may be more difficult – or impossible – for your sponsor to put you on an appropriate sponsorship scheme. Don't despair. If they were sufficiently impressed by you to give you a sponsorship in the first place, they may well be able to accommodate your needs. Otherwise, you may just have to part company. Whatever you do, be frank and upfront about your change of heart – and the sooner the better, before too much time and money are wasted.

---

## Fact check

Average starting salary paid to a 21-year-old graduate with a second-class Honours degree in 1997 was £15,500pa. Anticipated figure for 1998 is £16,000.

Law practices pay graduates the highest starting salaries in the UK: £20,000pa (1997 average figure).

233,300 first degree home students – a record number – graduated from higher education institutions in the UK in 1997.

It is estimated that 50% of sponsored students start their working careers with their sponsor.

Over 450 firms in the UK are thought to offer sponsorships.

150,000 approx students in the UK are enrolled on sandwich courses (1997–98 figure).

Sponsorship and work placement opportunities are increasing.

---

# SPONSORSHIP CASE STUDIES

## *Sponsorship with ICI*

Sponsored students have a choice of spending a pre-university 2–12 months with ICI – the length of training is specified by them, or undertaking a year's placement during their degree course; the pre-university salary is £6240 for the year. Either way all students undertake eight-week vacation placements in the summer. They are paid during the work placements, currently £180 a week plus accommodation, and receive a bursary £1650pa.

David Andrew, 20, in his first year of an Engineering degree at Durham, talks about his sponsorship with ICI.

*'My best decision was accepting an ICI sponsorship; my second, doing a pre-university year. It was planned right down to the last detail. The nine sponsored students – five guys and four girls – started off together on a week's personal learning skills course – a kind of unlocking your brains training with tips on speed reading and how to assimilate information quickly. We then spent three months on a practical workshop course learning lathing, milling etc, interspersed with academic work in maths,*

*electronics and engineering theory. We were living in three houses provided by ICI, fending for ourselves and having a lot of fun.*

*'So it wasn't until after Christmas when I joined the maintenance crew on a plant overhaul, that I got my first taste of work and responsibility. This was followed by a month in the design office, two weeks of Industrial Business Seminars down at Imperial College in London, a fantastic week on an "outward bound" type course in Yorkshire, and a crash course in German leading up to a two-week visit to Germany to compare the social, cultural and industrial differences between our two countries.*

*'At the beginning of the year we had to set ourselves a project to assist the disabled. My group of four chose to make an automatic feeding system for a girl with cerebral palsy. As she couldn't use her arms, it had to be a machine she could operate with her head. It was an ambitious idea, but it worked and we have definitely improved her way of life and her independence. When we handed it over, the local press and TV were there.*

*'Now at university I realise my sponsorship experience has given me a lot more understanding of my actual course. When others say: What's the point of this? What has it got to do with engineering? I just think it's got a lot.'*

## Sponsorship with APV Baker Ltd

Vanessa Leach studied Electronic and Electrical Engineering at Bradford University. She gained sponsorship with APV Baker, makers of processing machinery for the food processing industry, and undertook a pre-university industrial training year when she was paid £9,000. She then returned to the company during the summer vacations for 12 weeks and earned approximately £2280 in the first year and £2430–£2620 the next. She also received a bursary while studying of £1100 the first year, £1200 the second and £1300 in the third. She was then offered a job with the company at £15,850 a year.

*'The company said you can have the sponsorship providing you get into university. The university said I had to get at least three Cs in my A-levels, but I got one B and two Es; I was in danger of losing everything, until Bradford said they would take me anyway.*

*'My industrial training year was to be spent in Peterborough – my first time away from home – and I loved every minute of it. Lots of freedom and lots of money to spend. The company found us digs which was great, but I soon wanted more independence and three of us moved into our own house.*

'There were eight sponsored students – six boys and two girls. The year covered basic engineering training, two projects and a number of business seminars. It was the most incredible fun, but also hard work.

'I had decided to be an engineer because I liked playing with electrical things and making lights flash. Now I was to get my first chance of an engineering project. With two other sponsored students we were to design and build a nut dropper. The objective was to get the nuts on top of sweets. It was a novel machine – certainly the way we built it – and though some of the sweets looked a bit squashed, it did actually work. It was a tremendous learning experience and the chance to take responsibility for your own work.

'During the year I bought myself a computer, and at the end a little car, which I've found invaluable up here in Bradford where walking the streets at night alone is not recommended.

I loved work and couldn't wait to get back. So the next year I did an Easter placement as well. I helped in the demonstration area where customers come to test out their products on our machines. I then moved into Customer Training: dealing with the customers, updating manuals for machinery and showing the customers how processes worked. This was for me. And that's the job I shall return to after my finals.

'My bursary is almost exactly the same as the current student loan. So with my grant I am living on what most students can get and it is just about enough. I also have a four-hour Saturday job at Argos which brings in another £24 a week. I do it to help me relax, but it also provides a few luxuries.'

# 5
# OTHER SOURCES TO TAP

## Trusts, charitable awards, scholarships, bursaries, competitions

In this chapter we investigate all the other legitimate sources of finance you could tap to raise extra cash, and how to set about approaching them. They include trusts, charitable awards, scholarships, bursaries, and competitions.

## Other sources of finance: a reality or a vain hope?

You are right to be a little sceptical. If there were a prodigious number of organisations all eager to hand out money to students, you wouldn't have seen so many student demonstrations called to highlight their financial plight. But there are a surprising number of educational charities, trust funds and foundations, professional bodies, and benevolent funds available in this country which offer financial help to students. This may take the form of a scholarship or charitable award. One directory of

| Fast facts on alternative sources of finance | |
|---|---|
| Who gives bursaries and scholarships | Charitable trusts, universities and colleges, professional bodies and institutions |
| How much? | From £17 to £2000 and everything in between |
| Will an award affect my grant? | No |
| What is the success rate? | Low |

grant-making trusts we consulted listed over 1500 organisations under the broad heading of Education. But before you get too excited and think you've found the route to a crock of gold, when you start sifting through the many restrictions which trusts generally have to abide by, you soon realise there are relatively few – if any – that could meet your exact needs.

## What is a scholarship?

Scholarships differ from sponsorships by providing money while you study without the industrial training. They can, of course, be for a specific purpose like travel, to fund some special area of research, or possibly to study abroad. They are usually, though not always, given by institutions – this could be your university, a professional institute or a charitable trust – rather than by individual companies.

Competition is keen. Awards can be made on grounds of academic achievement or need. Whatever the criteria, they are not going to come your way without considerable effort and often disappointment, so be prepared. Nobody gives money away easily.

## What is a charitable award?

The difference between a scholarship and a charitable award is very indistinct, and you could say there is no difference at all, as charitable awards can often be scholarships. Charitable awards are always paid out by a charitable organisation which must abide by the terms and conditions of the original endowment. So however good and reasonable your case may be, if the money has to be paid out to a student from Gloucester studying Chemistry, it is no good being an Arts student from Leeds. To claim an award, both you and your financial predicament must fit the charity's help profile.

## What kind of awards are available?

Often the payments are small – to buy books, or equipment – but they can be quite substantial and cover fees or maintenance. So it could be from a few hundred pounds to a few thousand. They can be one-off payments, or given each year for the duration of your course.

# FINDING OUT ABOUT TRUSTS AND SCHOLARSHIPS

## Can my school help me?

Yes, most schools will have a list of local charities which offer help to students. The fact that you have been to the school could be a condition of receiving a grant. Also try your primary school. It is a good idea to find out if such scholarships and bursaries are available before you send off your UCAS application, as these sometimes stipulate a certain higher education establishment.

## Can my local authority help?

They should have details of any local charities which offer help to students in higher education.

## *Try also*

- The Welsh Office – they offer bursaries to Welsh-born students attending Welsh universities.

- The Carnegie Trust for the Universities of Scotland, which provides financial assistance to students of Scottish birth or extraction, or with at least two years' secondary education in Scotland, wanting to attend Scottish universities. They also offer vacation scholarships to enable undergraduates to undertake a research project during the long vacation. Contact Carnegie Trust for the Universities of Scotland, Cameron House, Abbey Park Place, Dunfermline, Fife KY12 7PZ. Tel: 0138 362 2148.

- The Scottish Education Department maintains a Register of Educational Endowments on Scottish trusts, many of which are local and open only to Scottish-born students wanting to attend Scottish universities. The Educational Department will search the Register on behalf of any student who submits an enquiry form. Forms are available from The Scottish Office Education Department, Students' Award Branch, Gyleview House, 3 Redheughs Rigg, Edinburgh EH12 9HH. Tel: 0131 244 5871.

# Check out your parents' employers!

Or at least get them to. A surprising number of companies and large employers have special trusts set up to help with the education of their employees' or past employees' children. Typical examples:

- The Miners' Welfare National Education Fund for dependants of those working in the coal-mining industry.

- The National Police Fund, which helps the children of people who are serving in or have served in the police force.

- The Royal Medical Benevolent Fund, which helps the children of medical graduates, and the Dain Fund Charities Committee (contact the BMA), which helps the children of registered members of the medical profession.

- The Royal Pinner School Foundation, which helps the children of sales representatives.

# Do universities and colleges give scholarships?

Some higher education institutions are endowed by generous benefactors and can award scholarships and bursaries to selected students who meet the required criteria. Usually an institution will have a very mixed bag of awards which bears very little relation to its academic strengths and interests. Most establishments don't give many awards, and competition is generally keen. Drop in the ocean or not, it is certainly worth a try. Many of the scholarships have a subject or location condition attached, which does considerably limit those eligible to apply.

# How much would a college scholarship be worth?

Awards vary in amounts tremendously: some are given annually for the full three to four years of a course, while others are a one-off payment. The highest awards seem to be around £2000 and the lowest we discovered was at Aberystwyth, for just £17.50. This, the university explained, was because the foundation was made in the 19th century and its status could not be changed. However no full scholarship there is less than £400.

# How would I go about getting a college scholarship?

Scholarship distribution methods differ with each institution and, of course, the terms of the foundation. Aberystwyth, for example, holds formal examinations during January each year. These can be taken at the student's own school or college. It gives 35–40 entry scholarships worth between £400 and £1000 a year. Entries need to be in by 15 December and scholars receive unconditional offers in March of the year of entry. Up to 150 merit awards of £300 and an unconditional offer are also given to candidates who do well in the examinations but who narrowly fail to gain a scholarship. Music bursaries are also available including a new one in honour of the 125th anniversary of the university.

The ancient Scottish universities all offer a range of bursaries – those at Glasgow are allocated once students are on courses, but at Aberdeen, Edinburgh and St Andrews scholarships are available to entrants from school. The number and value vary but there are quite a few worth £1000 a year (£4000 for a typical Scottish Honours degree or £5000 for a medical degree). Aberdeen has the largest number of bursaries in proportion to the size of the university, and in all cases the bursaries may be held in any faculty. Until 1998 school leavers sat examinations for bursaries, but the university is currently changing its system. Look for details in their prospectus or phone the university direct.

First look in the college prospectus – it should either list the awards given, or give you an address to write to for details. This should be done early in the autumn term of your final school year and before or about the time you are filling in your UCAS form. Obviously at this stage you do not know which university you are likely to go to, and any exam can be held early in the academic year, before you have made your final decision.

# What about the professional institutions? Do they give scholarships?

Some do, some don't. The engineering institutions are among the most generous. Awards are made to students studying IEE-accredited degree courses:

- Institution of Electrical Engineers (IEE), Savoy Place, London WC2R 0BL. Tel: 0171 240 1871: give 35 scholarships of £750pa for the duration of the degree course, 20 of which are for women.

- Institution of Civil Engineers, 1–7 Great George Street, London SW1 3AA. Tel: 0171 222 7722. The Queens Jubilee Scholarship Trust awards some 30 scholarships a year valued at £1250pa paid for the duration of the degree course; the Board of Incorporated Engineers and Technicians Award fund (BSAF) awards some 10 scholarships worth up to £500 plus a number of smaller awards.

- Paper Federation of Great Britain, Papermakers House, Rivenhall Road, Westlea, Swindon SN5 7BD. Tel: 01793 886086. Rackley Scholarship £1000pa for duration of the course, usually three given to undergraduates at UMIST. About half Paper Science undergraduates receive company sponsorship worth up to £2800pa plus pay for holiday work and every Paper Science undergraduate not receiving a scholarship or sponsorship will get a Paper Industry Bursary of £500pa.

- Institution of Mechanical Engineers, Northgate Avenue, Bury St Edmunds, Suffolk IP32 6BN. Tel: 01284 718617: Whitworth Scholarships – up to 10 awarded, currently valued at £3000 a year for length of course, given to engineers taking a degree who left full-time education at an early age, generally 16; James Clayton Undergraduate Scholarship, up to 10 given each year, £1500 paid out over three years at £500 a year.

- Company of Chartered Surveyors, 16 St Mary-at-Hill, London EC3R 8EE; Tel: 0171 623 2761: offer assistance to students of between £250 and £1000 for extreme financial hardship, ie students who could not finish the course without help in their final year of a first degree course in surveying.

- Institute of Marine Engineers, The Memorial Building, 76 Mark Lane, London EC3R 7JN. Tel: 0171 481 8493. Up to 10 scholarships of £1000 are awarded each year to students attending approved accredited courses who demonstrate a commitment to maritime engineering by at least two years in the industry or in study. Also administers the Wavespec Marine Engineering Scholarship Scheme which offers a further three awards of £1000 each year to mature students on accredited courses.

- The Mineral Industries Educational Trust, 6 St James's Square, London SW1Y 4LD. Tel: 0171 753 2117. Awards are given to students studying honours degrees in mining, quarrying, mineral processing, extractive metallurgy, and applied geology. Some MSc courses are also sponsored. Bursaries: £1250pa, with exceptional students gaining scholarships of £1750pa. Postgraduates £2000pa.

- The Institute of Materials, 1 Carlton House Terrace, London SW1Y 5DB runs a £1000 bursary scheme awarded to students interested in materials science/engineering for their first year at university. For a list of accredited degrees, careers booklet, video and full details phone 0171 839 4071.

## What charities and trusts help students, and how would I get in touch with them?

In the next few pages we list some of the charitable organisations where you could apply for financial help. This is by no means an exhaustive list, but it will give you a head start. Addresses and more details can be found in the directories listed here, which should be available in your local library.

### Books to read

- *The Grants Register*, published by Macmillan.
- *Directory of Grant-Making Trusts*, published by the Charities Aid Foundation.
- *The Educational Grants Directory* published by the Directory of Social Change.
- *Charities Digest*, published by the Family Welfare Association.
- *Money to Study*, published by the Family Welfare Association.

### Advice note

Before making an application to a charity, it is important to be clear in your own mind exactly what kind of student they are likely to help, and what kind of financial assistance you are after, otherwise you could be wasting both your own time and theirs.

# TRUSTS AND CHARITIES FOR DISABLED STUDENTS

Arthritis Care
British Association of Health Services in Higher Education
Drapers' Charitable Fund
The Peter Greenwood Memorial Trust for the Deaf or Hearing Impaired
Institution of Electrical Engineers – The Lord Hirst Fund
Mary MacArthur Educational Trust
The Hilda Martindale Educational Trust
Royal National Institute for the Blind
Royal National Institute for Deaf People
Snowdon Award Scheme

# TRUSTS AND CHARITIES FOR THOSE STUDYING SPECIFIC SUBJECTS

ACCOUNTANCY
  Association of Certified Accountants: Certified Accountant's Jubilee
  Scholarships
AERONAUTICS
  Royal Aeronautical Society
AGRICULTURE
  The William Scott Abbott Trust
  Douglas Bomford Trust
  Royal Bath & West Southern Counties Society Travelling
  Scholarships
ARCHITECTURE
  Architects' Registration Council of the United Kingdom
CHEMISTRY
  Royal Society of Chemistry Marriott Bequest Scheme
COMMERCE/COMPUTER/BUSINESS STUDIES
  Koettgen Memorial Fund
DENTISTRY
  General Dental Council Charitable Trust

LAW
  Bar Council Students' Loan Fund and The Bar Council's Trust
  Funds Committee
  Chambers Pupillage Awards
  The Council of Legal Education Inns of Court Studentships
  Law Society Bursary and Loan Schemes
  Solicitors Benevolent Association
MEDICINE
  Lord Ashdown Charitable Trust
  BMA Medical Education Trust
MUSIC
  Benslow Musical Instrument Loan Scheme
  Gerald Finzi Charitable Trust
  Martin Musical Scholarship Fund
  Royal Society of Musicians of Great Britain
MUSIC, DRAMA, VISUAL ARTS
  Berkwickshire Educational Trust
  Bird's Charity – Royal Academy of Arts
PHARMACISTS
  The Royal Pharmaceutical Society's Benevolent Fund
SCIENCE AND ENGINEERING
  The Caroline Haslett Memorial Trust (mainly to women)
  Students' Aid Fund – Institution of Mechanical Engineers
  Worshipful Company of Scientific Instrument Makers
  Worshipful Company of Shipwrights (maritime subjects)

## What sort of help do trusts give?

Help with fees, maintenance, books, equipment, travel either to and
from your college or abroad, special sports activities, childminding,
special projects. They all vary in what they will offer, and to whom.

## Is there anybody who could advise me on applying to charitable trusts?

EGAS, which stands for the Education Grants Advisory Service, is an
independent organisation which will advise students on organisations to
contact. They have a comprehensive database of charities and trusts. If
you write to them, setting out briefly your financial predicament and
needs, they will dip into their extensive files and see who are the most

likely bodies to help you. With their list of names and addresses comes a helpful leaflet on how to approach charities. The agency mainly helps students who are not eligible for statutory funding. Those who do receive statutory funding and apply must have explored other alternatives first such as the Access Funds and student loans. Generally EGAS is not able to help postgraduates except in exceptional circumstances. Write enclosing a stamped addressed envelope to EGAS, 501–505 Kingsland Road, Dalston, London E8 4AU or telephone the information line on 0717 245 6251.

# What are my chances of hitting the jackpot?

Your chances are slim, though the odds are certainly better than the likelihood of winning the national lottery. Competition is fierce. EGAS receives well over 16,000 written applications a year.

EGAS does in fact offer a number of small grants itself to students for particular needs. These are usually small – up to £200 – and for something specific like a computer or equipment for a hairdressing course. They handle about 40 grants a month and most are given to help students in their final year. Typical examples:

- for books or equipment
- a parent is suddenly made redundant and can't continue to finance fees
- a student, who has been paying their way through part-time work, feels they need to give it up for that final two month push.

*Last word:* Be realistic when contacting EGAS. Don't expect miracles, they can rarely be worked.

# When should I contact a trust?

Most trusts have an application deadline. This is usually given along with the information in the trust and grants directories. Check out each entry carefully; they are all different. Trusts are not the answer for a fast financial fix. Like all bodies, they tend to move exceedingly slowly. Your case would have to be scrutinised along with many others, so it could be months before you get an answer.

## Could I get through higher education funded only by a charitable trust?

It could be done, but don't depend on it. Many charities won't consider you until you have tried all the usual channels available to students, and they do tend to give help towards the end of a course, rather than the beginning.

## If I get help from a charity, will it affect my grant?

No. Charitable awards and scholarships, like sponsorships, will not affect your grant, and are unlikely to bring your finances into the tax bracket.

## Can I apply to more than one charity?

Yes, but blanket saturation is not advisable. Limit your applications to organisations which are really likely to give you funds.

## How do I go about applying to a charity?

There are no set rules. What one charitable trust wants, another doesn't. Here is a general procedure to follow:

1. Put together a list of suitable charities *either* by consulting the list in this book, EGAS, or the directories in the library.
2. Find out exactly what each charity is offering by consulting the directories listed earlier in this chapter. Check if there is any date by which your entry must be in.
3. Write a brief note to the charities you consider most suitable, explaining your need and asking for any details about the charity, and if they have an application form.
4. Photocopy any application form you are sent before starting to fill it in so that you can have a dummy run. A form full of crossings-out does not create the best impression.
5. Fill in the application form. Make sure your answers are clear and truthful. You may be questioned on it later. There will probably be a section asking you to give details of why you are in need of financial assistance. Try to be concise without missing out any relevant facts. Bear the trust's criteria in mind.

6. Photocopy the completed form before you send it back. You need to know exactly what you have said, and the details may be useful for subsequent forms.

7. Wait patiently. These things can take many weeks to process.

## Do students actually get help?

*'As an Engineering student I needed a computer, but couldn't afford one. Were there any charities that could help? I searched around, and discovered the Earl's Colne Educational Trust, which assisted students living within ten miles of Earl's Colne in Essex. I lived in Halstead, just within the limits – it was worth a try. I wrote to them explaining my needs; they sent me a form; I filled it in; I waited; I went for an interview. The result: £500 – easy money. It cost just two sides of A4!'* Jonathan Wilson, when studying Electronic Engineering at Loughborough University

## COMPETITIONS – A WORTHWHILE OPTION?

Competitions are not a very reliable or constant source of -nance, but again you may be lucky. Occasionally companies or newspapers will run competitions. The prize can be money, books, travel, or the chance to work abroad for that company. They are usually one-off opportunities.

If it's a competition set especially for students, it very often involves writing an essay. Students, being the overworked (or is it lazy?) people they are, tend to give them a miss, so the number of entries can be poor. All the more reason to give it a try.

Several years ago the Chartered Accountancy firm KPMG ran such a competition, and seven lucky undergraduates won the chance to work for six weeks for the firm in such faraway places as São Paulo, Toronto, Cologne, Melbourne, Sydney, Harare and Tai Pei. They were given an open airfare ticket which gave them a chance to travel, earned six weeks' salary and invaluable work experience. Not bad for a few hours' work on a 1500-word essay.

*The Independent* ran a travel writing competition in conjunction with Fodor's the publishers. The first prize was a round-the-world air ticket, plus spending money, all for a 1000-word article.

New students applying for a student account with NatWest can get their FREE money management guide which includes a free prize draw. Not exactly a competition, but you are in with a chance.

Occasionally there are competitions held within universities. Aberystwyth, for example, holds a Student Skills Competition. This is a unique event which sets out to help students recognise the skills they have already acquired. The final involves small teams of students designing exhibition stands for the Careers Information Fair and this year for the first time they were helped by local employers. The first prize is £500 – not a vast fortune if you are a large team, but the experience, we are told, is great fun.

The drawback with competitions is that the winner takes all and the many also-rans get nothing. Still, it's worth keeping your eyes open.

## Where to look

- On your college noticeboard
- In the careers office
- National newspapers
- Student newspapers.

# 6

# TIGHTEN YOUR BELTS

## Funding for postgraduates

Postgraduates are proliferating. In the last ten years the number of students on postgraduate courses has almost doubled. How are they managing to pay for their studies? Has funding kept pace with the demand? In this chapter we look at the main sources of finance for postgraduates.

## How many postgraduates are there?

According to a survey commissioned by the DfEE there were 352,000 students on full-time postgraduate courses in the UK in 1996–97. Today the figure is probably higher.

## Which are the boom areas for postgraduate study?

The biggest growth has been in university Masters courses especially in medicine-related degrees, business MBAs and computing-based courses. Social sciences and the humanities are also increasing in popularity. Lowest rise is in engineering and technology.

## Is it worth taking a postgraduate qualification?

Yes, if it's a subject you are particularly interested in or if it is a vocational course, and certainly if you are seeking a post in academia or a research-based organisation. But there is no real evidence to suggest that in general further qualifications will help you secure a job.

# How much will it cost?

**Tuition Fees**

*UK Residents and EU Nationals*
Maximum fee 1998–99 – £2610pa
Certain courses may be higher: Legal Practice Course £5000pa up to
MBA £10,000.

*Students from abroad*
Average for 1998–99
| | |
|---|---|
| Arts | £6300 |
| Science | £8200 |
| Clinical | £15,400 |

**Maintenance**
The results of our research given in Chapter 1 will give you some idea.
However, standards for postgraduates tend to be higher. The British
Council is currently telling overseas students wanting to study in the
UK that they would need at least £7000–£9000 to live in London and
£6000–£8000 in other parts of the country with additional expenses of
£300–£500 for books and equipment.

# Will I get funding?

Don't bank on it. Competition for funding for postgraduates is phenomenal. There is no all–embracing funding system as for first degrees and
students generally have to search around to get help. It is much easier to
get a place on a course than it is to get the money to pay for it. Many
postgraduates have to finance themselves with loans etc, which is probably why part-time study for postgraduates is increasing in popularity. If
you are offered funding make sure it covers both tuition fees and
maintenance.

# When should I start considering taking a
postgraduate course?

At least a year before you graduate.

# What are the possible sources for funding?

1. **Government Funding from Research Councils and the British Academy** – These are by far the largest sources of funding in the UK. Some 9000 new awards are made each year. Each 'awarding body' funds different courses and there is no overlap, so it is important to identify the appropriate body for your needs (see this chapter; see page 167 for Scotland & Northern Ireland).

2. **SOCRATES ERASMUS** – Programme developed by the European Commission to provide funds for the mobility of students and staff in universities throughout the EU member states and the countries of the European Free Trade Association (EFTA). See page 52 for full details and information on Leonardo.

3. **Employers** – Employers will occasionally sponsor employees through courses, especially MBAs.

4. **Companies** – May sponsor students on a research project. This could be as the result of a work experience association during a first degree, or in cooperation with one of the research councils.

5. **Trusts and Charities** – More likely to award small amounts of money rather than full financial support, but certainly worth considering. (See Chapter 5 Other Sources to Tap.) Your Local Authority Awards Officer would have details of any local charities. Otherwise contact EGAS (see page 149 for details) or look in the published charities and grant-making trusts directories and registers. Apply early, processing can be inordinately slow.

6. **Local authorities** – Except in the case of teacher training, local authorities are not required by law to fund postgraduates. Funding is discretionary, is given mainly for vocational courses which lead to certificates or diplomas, is means tested and criteria differ between authorities. Likely subjects are accountancy, journalism, law, music, secretarial work, youth work, computing. If you are tapping your local authority it is essential to apply early as their funds are limited, and you'll need to put up a good case for yourself. But, because there are no set rules for funding, it is always worth a try. Applications should be made by March/April.

7. **Universities' own postgraduate studentship awards** – Many institutions have a small number of studentships available for specific courses. Aberystwyth for example gives about 10 awards in total which could be for one or three years for research degrees. Awards cover fees and maintenance. Closing date for applications

May 1st (Arts and Humanities), June 1st (Sciences). Check your university of choice for details.

8. **University departments** – They may have nothing, and probably won't advertise. But, if they particularly want you, or there's something they are interested in doing, they may have sources they can tap. You could find they stipulate that you have to take on some tutorial work or assist the department.

   Tip from Gina Preston of Aberystwyth's Postgraduate Admissions Office: 'I say to graduates its always worth a try, all it needs is the right phone call just at the right time'.

9. **Research Assistantships** – These are salaried posts in academic departments which provide the opportunity to study for a higher degree. Salaries vary and opportunities can become available throughout the year. Watch the relevant press for adverts – *Guardian*, *Times*, *New Scientist*, *Nature* etc.

10. **Loans from banks** – See later in this chapter.

## Can I get a student loan?

Only if you are taking a Postgraduate Certificate in Education (PGCE). *Plus point*: even though it's generally only a one year course, you will be classed as a first rather than a final year student so can take out the maximum loan offered and you won't have to pay fees. Otherwise NO. Try a bank loan (see page 176).

## Who exactly are the award-making bodies?

These are the main sources of government funding for postgraduates. There are some nine major award-making bodies in the UK. Each one operates independently and the awards they offer are all slightly different, as are their regulations. The information given here should, therefore, be seen as a general guide to what you could expect to get. All the award-making bodies issue information about their own awards which can be gained by writing, or phoning them individually (addresses are given later in this chapter) or looking on the Internet. The areas of study covered by individual Research Councils can change, so make sure any information you get is up to date.

# What kind of government award could I get?

Basically there are four kinds of awards for postgraduate students:

- A Research Studentship, which is generally a three-year award leading to a doctorate (PhD or DPhil).

- A Collaborative Research Studentship, when the research project is part-funded by an outside industrial organisation and may well give the student some experience outside the academic environment. The collaborating company generally gives the student extra cash on top of the studentship award. The awarding body may also give an additional £350 on top of the basic studentship. This is certainly the situation with CASE (Cooperative Awards in Science and Engineering) students.

- Advanced Course Studentships, which are given for taught courses which must be of at least six months' duration, but are generally for one year, often leading to a Masters (MSc, MA) or other qualification.

- Bursaries, which are allocated by the British Academy to selected institutions for selected postgraduate courses – largely professional or vocational. The institution then nominates the candidate for the award (see page 167 for allocating bodies for Scotland and Northern Ireland).

Not all awarding bodies give all types of award. And some give additional awards and fellowships.

# Is the award means-tested?

It depends on the body. Some awards are means tested on parents' or spouse's income, some on spouse's income alone and some not at all.

# What could an award cover?

- payment of approved fees to the institution
- maintenance allowance
- dependants' and other allowances
- assistance with additional travel and subsistence expenses for something like fieldwork.

# Do I have to get a 2:1 to take a postgraduate course?

Each course will set its own requirements. If you are thinking of specialising in your degree subject, a 1st or 2:1 is probably what you will need. For a vocational course, you'll need to show real commitment and interest in the subject. If, however, you are seeking funding from a government funding council, they will generally demand:

- a first or upper-second class honours degree or a lower-second with a further qualification such as an MA for a Research Studentship
- at least a lower-second honours degree for a taught/one year course. (This does not apply to Social Work courses.)

## How do I go about getting funding?

Start with your university careers office. Most are very on the ball when it comes to tapping the meagre resources available to postgraduates. They may even publish a special leaflet on sources of funding for postgraduate study. Many of the publications listed at the end of this chapter, which we suggest you consult, should also be in the university careers library. Talk also to the tutors in your department, especially if you are wanting to undertake a research degree, as they will know what projects are likely to gain funding. Consult university prospectuses.

## When should I approach the award-making bodies?

If you want general information on their award scheme – any time. It is important to read thoroughly the individual information produced by the different award-making bodies as their closing dates, methods of application and what they offer will vary. In most cases application for awards is done through the institution you hope to join. Check information for procedure.

## How do I apply for funding?

In the case of most research councils (BBSRC, EPSRC, MRC, NERC, PPARC), funding to students is funnelled through university departments and courses. They select the students for their courses/projects and submit their names to the awarding body. Application forms are obtained from the department for your intended studies and must be returned to them well in advance of July 31st when the department will submit it to the appropriate awarding council.

In the case of the British Academy and Economic and Social Research Council (ESRC), awards are allocated by competition. Having secured an offer of a place on a course, students apply for an award through their referees. Applications must be with the appropriate awarding body by May 1st, so again make sure your application is with your course 'organisers' long before then.

## Will it make a difference where I choose to study?

Yes. Not all courses or departments attract funding. It is important to find out the situation when you apply. And just because a course is eligible for studentships, and you have a place on that course, it still doesn't mean you will necessarily get one. It is very competitive. And remember, if you don't get funding it could mean not only paying your own maintenance but also course fees. Then, a university close to your own home might be the answer, or studying part-time (day release, evening courses or distance learning).

## When and how can I find out what projects have funding?

From April onwards your university should have a list of university departments that have been given funding by the awarding bodies. Under the scheme, universities are committed to attracting the very best students for the awards, so must advertise for candidates outside as well as inside their own university. Typical media: *New Scientist, Nature, The Guardian*, university magazines depending on the topic. If you want a list of which courses and projects throughout the country have received funding, contact the appropriate awarding body after April 1st.

## Can I approach more than one awarding body?

No. There is no overlap between the awarding research councils; they each have their designated topics they fund. So, it is important to identify which body to apply to as you can only apply to one. In the case of the British Academy there does appear to be some overlap between its three different arms. However, a course which attracts bursaries from one will not generally gain funding from other state sources.

## THE AWARD-MAKING BODIES

Figures quoted are for 1997–98 unless stated. They are all per annum. Subjects given for each body have been selected to give a broad view of topics covered and are by no means exhaustive. Candidates should check with the appropriate organisation, or on the appropriate website.

BIOTECHNOLOGY AND BIOLOGICAL SCIENCES RESEARCH COUNCIL (BBSRC) – part of the Science and Engineering Research Council.

Subject areas:  Agricultural engineering, animal sciences, biochemical engineering, biochemistry, biomaterials science, biomolecular sciences, bioprocessing engineering, cell biology, development biology, genetics, human diet and health microbiology, neurobiology and psychology, plant sciences, soil sciences, veterinary sciences.

Type of award:  Research Studentship
Advanced Course Studentship
Veterinary Research Fellowship

Amount

| | standard | | special |
|---|---|---|---|
| | year 1 and 2 | 3rd year | |
| Study in London | £6840 | £7340 | £8700 |
| Elsewhere | £5510 | £6010 | £6820 |

For students with a recognised veterinary degree £14,280

(NB: CASE awards – additional £350 given by Council plus minimum £2355 by collaborator)

Address:  Biotechnology and Biological Sciences Research Council
Polaris House
North Star Avenue
Swindon SN2 1UH
Tel: 01793 413200
web: www.bbsrc.ac.uk

## ECONOMIC AND SOCIAL RESEARCH COUNCIL (ESRC)

Subject areas: Area studies, economics, economic and social history, education, human geography, linguistics, management and business studies (accounting, finance, industrial relations and other specialist management courses), planning, politics and international relations, psychology, social anthropology, social administration, socio-legal studies, sociology, social statistics, womens studies methods and computing applied to the social sciences.

Type of award: Research Studentship
Advanced Course Studentship

Amount: Studying in London                    £6855
Elsewhere                              £5295

Address: Economic and Social Research Council
Postgraduate Training Division
Polaris House
North Star Avenue
Swindon SN2 1UJ
Tel: 01793 413096
web: http://www.esrc.ac/ptd/comp/comp.htm

## MEDICAL RESEARCH COUNCIL (MRC)

Subject areas: Medicine (including tropical), areas of biology including molecules and cells, inheritance, reproduction and child health, infections and immunity (including HIV and AIDS), cancer, imaging, neurobiology, cognitive science, clinical neurosciences and mental health, health services research, clinical psychology.

Type of award: Research Studentships (including Collaborative Studentships)

| Amount: | | 1st year | 2nd year | 3rd year |
|---|---|---|---|---|
| | Study in London: | £9122 | £9570 | £10,027 |
| | Elsewhere | £6865 | £7268 | £7676 |

Type of award: Advanced Course Studentships (Standard)

| | Study in London: | £8900 |
|---|---|---|
| | Elsewhere | £6700 |

Type of award: Research Masters Studentships (MRes)

| | Study in London: | £9122 |
|---|---|---|
| | Elsewhere | £6865 |

NB Collaborative Studentship – additional money may be awarded to students by collaborative partner.

Address:    Medical Research Council
20 Park Crescent
London W1N 4AL
Tel: 0171 636 5422
web: http://www.mrc.ac.uk

## NATURAL ENVIRONMENT RESEARCH COUNCIL (NERC)

Subject areas:    Geology, organic pollution, geophysics, physical oceanography, marine ecology, hydrology, freshwater ecology, terrestrial ecology, soil sciences, earth observation and associated science, atmospheric chemistry, science based archaeology.

Type of award:    Research Studentship
Co-operative Award in Science and Engineering (CASE)
Advance Course Studentship

Amount:    Study in London    £6835
Elsewhere    £5510
NB CASE Award – additional £350 given by council.

Address:    Natural Environment Research Council
Polaris House
North Star Avenue
Swindon SN2 1UH
Tel: 01793 411500
web: http://www.nerc.ac.uk

## ENGINEERING AND PHYSICAL SCIENCES RESEARCH COUNCIL (EPSRC)

Subject areas:    Chemistry, mathematics, physics (other than that assigned to PPARC, but including nuclear structure physics), information technology, manufacturing technology, materials science, design, control instrumentation, clean technology, computer science and engineering.

Type of award:    Research Studentship
Cooperative Awards in Science and Engineering (CASE)
Advanced Course Studentship

| Amount: | Studying in London | £7060 |
| (1998–99) | Elsewhere | £5455 |

(NB CASE awards – additional £350 given by Council plus minimum of £2500 by collaborator)

Address:   Engineering and Physical Sciences Research Council
Polaris House
North Star Avenue
Swindon SN2 1ET
Tel: 01793 444000
web: http://www.epsrc.ac.uk

## PARTICLE PHYSICS AND ASTRONOMY RESEARCH COUNCIL (PPARC)

Subject areas:   Astronomy, planetary science, particle physics.
Type of award:   Research Studentship
Cooperative Award in Science and Engineering (CASE)
Advanced Course Studentship

| Amount: | Studying in London | £6855 |
| | Elsewhere | £5295 |

NB CASE Award – additional £350 given by Council plus minimum of £2355 by collaborator).

Address:   Particle Physics and Astronomy Research Council
Polaris House
North Star Avenue
Swindon SN2 1UH
Tel: 01793 442118
web: http://www.pparc.ac.uk

## CENTRAL COUNCIL FOR EDUCATION AND TRAINING IN SOCIAL WORK (CCETSW)

Subject areas:   Social Work
Type of award:   Bursary for Diploma in Social Work

| Amount: | Studying in London | £3464 |
| | Elsewhere | £2724 |
| | Living in parents' home | £2034 |

NB award is means tested on parents'/spouses' income.

Address:   Central Council for Education and Training in Social Work
Information Service

Derbyshire House
St Chad's Street
London WC1H 8AD
Tel: 0171 278 2455
http://www.ccetsw.org.uk

Probationary Work – no postgraduate qualification needed. Suitable candidates are now recruited direct into the Probation Service as trainees and an individual training programme is implemented depending on previous experience.

For further information contact:
The Probation Training Unit
C6 Division
Home Office
50 Queen Anne's Gate
London SW1H 9AT
Tel: 0171 273 2675

## MINISTRY OF AGRICULTURE, FISHERIES AND FOOD (MAFF)

| | |
|---|---|
| Subject areas: | Agriculture, horticulture and farm management, agricultural science, agricultural engineering, agricultural economics |
| Type of award: | Research Studentship |
| | Cooperative Award in Science and Engineering (CASE) |
| | Advance Course Studentship |
| Amount: | Studying in London £7248 |
| | Elsewhere £5778 |
| | NB CASE awards collaborator may give additional funds to student £1370 but it is not mandatory. |
| Address: | Ministry of Agriculture, Fisheries & Food |
| | Room 734, St Christopher House, |
| | Southwark Street |
| | London SE1 OUD |
| | Tel: 0171 921 3885 |
| | Maff Helpline: 0645 335577 (local call rates) |
| | web: http://www.maff.gov.uk |

# THE BRITISH ACADEMY

## 1. Humanities Research Board

Subject areas:   English and American studies, media and
communication studies, other languages, literatures and
cultures, linguistics, visual and performing arts, history
of art and architecture, history, philosophy, history and
philosophy of science, theology, divinity and religious
studies, archaeology, classics and law

Type of award:   Doctoral Research Studentship

Amount:   Study in London                £6855
Elsewhere                            £5295

Address:   Postgraduate Studentships Office
Humanities Research Board
The British Academy
10 Carlton House Terrace
London SW1Y 5AH
Tel: 0171 969 5200
web: http://britac3.britac.ac.uk

## 2. Professional and Vocational Awards

Subject areas:   Library and information science.

Type of award:   Research Studentship 2 or 3 years
Research Fellowship 2 years
Advanced Course Studentship 6–12 months

Amount:   Course fees:                    £2540 max
Studying in London              £5590
Elsewhere                        £4760
Living with parents             £3505
(means-tested on parents'/spouses' income)

Address:   Professional and Vocational Awards
Humanities Research Board
The British Academy
10 Carlton House Terrace
London SW1Y 5AH
Tel: 0171 969 5200
web: http://britac3.britac.ac.uk

## 3. Bursaries

Type of course: Archaeology, archive administration, art and design,
interpreting and translating, practical theology, media
studies.

Type of award:   State Bursary
Amount:          Course fees                    £2540 max
                 Maintenance:
                 Studying in London             £3547
                 Elsewhere                      £2803
                 Living with parents            £2117
                 (means tested on parents'/spouses' income)
                 Address:
                 State Bursaries
                 Humanities Research Board
                 The British Academy
                 10 Carlton House Terrace
                 London SW1Y 5AH
                 Tel: 0171 969 5200
                 web: http://britac3.britac.ac.uk

**Scotland:** Graduates seeking funding for science-based subjects are eligible for studentship awards from most of the Research Councils mentioned here. For studentships and bursaries for the arts/humanities and postgraduate vocational training you should apply to the Students Awards Agency for Scotland, Gyleview House, 3 Redheughs Rigg, Edinburgh EH12 9HH. Tel: 0131 244 5848.

**Northern Ireland:** Funding is provided by three separate bodies.

1. The Northern Ireland Department of Agriculture for study in agriculture, horticulture and related sciences (closing date 28th Feb).
2. The Medical Research Council (see details for the UK).
3. The Department of Education for Northern Ireland (DENI), which provides studentships on a competitive basis for courses in humanities, science, technology, social sciences and natural environment studies. Application is through the department where you wish to study. Contact university for place Dec/Jan. Forms are available in March. DENI also provides bursaries for approved diploma and vocational courses.

*Booklet on awards available from the Department of Education for Northern Ireland.*

**Channel Islands/Isle of Man:** apply direct to appropriate education department.

# ADDITIONAL INFORMATION ON BURSARIES

## Do all postgraduate courses offer bursaries?

No, some courses don't qualify. And on courses that do, not all the students get a bursary because state bursaries are offered on a quota basis to educational institutions. Caution: courses funded at one institution may not be funded at another, even if they have the same or a similar name.

## How do I know if I will get a bursary?

When you apply for a course, ask if it is eligible for bursaries. If you are offered a place then make sure which of the following the offer includes:

(a) a firm nomination for a bursary
(b) inclusion on a reserve list for a bursary
(c) a course place with no bursary.

## What if I want to train as a teacher?

If you take a course leading to the Postgraduate Certificate in Education (PGCE) or specified equivalent, you will not have to pay any contribution towards your tuition fees. Like undergraduates, you will be able to apply for the reduced grant, which will be means-tested on parents'/spouse's income, and increased loan for 1998–99 and for just the increased loan from 1999–2000 onwards. This will also be means-tested. To encourage people into teaching in areas where there is a real shortage the DfEE has implemented the Secondary Subject Shortage Scheme whereby teacher training institutions can give an additional bursary based on financial need, to students taking an undergraduate or postgraduate teacher training in the following areas:

Sciences (physics, chemistry, biology or any combination)
Mathematics
Design and technology
Information technology
Modern foreign languages
Religious education
Music
Welsh.

The bursary is available to degree students and those on a one- or two-year PGCE course at a college/university that offers courses in the Secondary Subject Shortage areas listed. It is largely a hardship scheme with each individual institute setting their own criteria for offering the award. This is a new scheme which replaces the Priority Subject Recruitment Scheme.

To find out more about teaching as a career contact: Teacher Training Agency, Communications Centre, PO Box 3210 Chelmsford, Essex CM1 3WA. Tel: (England) 01245 454454; (Wales) 01222 825831.

## Fast Fact . . .

. . . for Welsh language speaking teachers. Under the Welsh Medium Incentive Support Scheme, PGCE students studying to teach any subject in Welsh can apply for a bursary of £1200pa. Sixty were given in 1997. Contact the Welsh Office Education Department, FHE1 Division, 4th Floor, Cathays Park, Cardiff CF1 3NQ. Tel: 01222 825831.

## TOP UP FUNDS

## Are there any other funds I can apply for?

Yes. But each council or funding body has devised their own additional allowance scheme. We have listed a number of them here, but you will find if you are entitled to, say, a Mature Student's Allowance, you will not be eligible for a Postgraduate Experience Allowance. So you will have to ask your funding council what they will provide.

**Mature Students Incentive Allowance**
£1430 given to students of 26 years and over
To be eligible for this you must be 26 in the April before you commence your studies.

**Allowance for Mature Students**
To claim you must be over 26, and have earned at least £12,000 in wages or received government benefits during the last three years:

| Age | pa |
|-----|-----|
| 26 | £330 |
| 27 | £580 |

| | |
|---|---|
| 28 | £860 |
| 29+ | £1130 |

## Postgraduate Experience Allowance

If you have worked for two years full-time in a job directly relevant to your first degree or proposed course and this includes at least one year since graduating you may qualify for a special allowance which in 1997–8 was:

| *Age* | *pa* |
|---|---|
| 22 years | £650 |
| 23 years | £1115 |
| 24 years | £1340 |
| 25 years | £1605 |
| 26 years | £1845 |
| 27 years or over | £2090 |

## Older Students Allowance

This if for students not eligible for the Postgraduate Experience Allowance who have supported themselves for at least two years.

| *Age* | *pa* |
|---|---|
| 23 | £650 |
| 24 | £880 |
| 25+ | £1130 |

*Alternative Allowance*

| | |
|---|---|
| | £650 |

## Bursary Students Allowance

You must be over 25 with at least two years' work experience.

| *Age* | *pa* |
|---|---|
| 26 | £330 |
| 27 | £580 |
| 28 | £860 |
| 29+ | £1130 |

# I have three kids and a husband to support – what help is there for me?

If you have been awarded a studentship or bursary and have a family to support then help is at hand. There are two types of schemes currently running. Eligibility will depend on your awarding body and current situation. Rates are for 1998 and may vary with different awarding bodies.

**Scheme 1**
**Young Dependants' Allowance (YDA)**
Must be single parent with sole financial responsibility for your child/ children

|  | pa |
|---|---|
| For first child under 18 years | £1735 |
| Second or other children | £1020 |
| Maximum award | £2755 |

**Scheme 2**
**Dependants' Allowance**

|  |  |
|---|---|
| Spouse or adult | £2025 |
| Children under 11 | £425 |
| aged 11–15 | £850 |
| aged 16–17 | £1120 |
| aged 18 or over | £1620 |

For a single parent £2025 is allowed for the first child and they may be able to claim an additional hardship allowance of £970–£1,000.

If you have to go away to study and so are keeping two homes you could also claim £700 housing maintenance.

# I am disabled – can I get extra help?

If you have a long-term disability for which you have been receiving financial support, you may be eligible for an extra allowance. Your funding body should be able to tell you.

As we go to press the government is still discussing whether to extend the student allowances for disabled undergraduates and PGCE students (see pages 81–82) to  cover all disabled postgraduate students. Check with your funding body, local education authority or the DfEE. Tel: 0171 825 5219 to see if a decision has been made. If it hasn't yet, check again next year.

QUICK CHECK

| Awards | In London | Elsewhere | Living at home |
|---|---|---|---|
| BBSRC | £6840–£8700 | £5510–£6820 | N/A |
| ERSC | £6855 | £5295 | N/A |
| MRC | £8900–£9122 | £6700–£6865 | N/A |
| NERC | £6835 | £5510 | N/A |
| EPSRC[1] | £7060 | £5455 | N/A |
| PPARC | £6855 | £5295 | N/A |
| CCETSW* | £3464 | £2724 | £2034 |
| MAFF | £7248 | £5778 | N/A |
| BA 1 Humanities | £6855 | £5295 | N/A |
| *2 Professional & Vocational | £5590 | £4760 | £3505 |
| *3 Bursaries | £3547 | £2803 | £2117 |
| PGCE*1 | £1225 | £810 | £480 |
| | (+£3145 loan) | (+£2735 loan) | (+£2325 loan) |

\* = means tested
[1] = figures for 1998/9. Other figures shown are 1997/8.

# Are funding arrangements the same for all parts of the UK?

No. For residents in Scotland, Northern Ireland, the Channel Islands and the Isle of Man, funding arrangements are slightly different.

# I want to study for the law – what help is there?

With course fees for the Common Professional Examination (CPE) £2700–£3500 and the Legal Practice Course (LPC) running at an average of £5000 – substantially more at top schools, most students are going to need some help.

**1. Sponsorship/training contract leading to Articles.** This is financially the best route. A firm providing sponsorship/a training contract would pay for your fees at law school for the one or two years, give a maintenance allowance and possibly vacation work. But sponsorship is competitive and even the best students can find it difficult to get. There are an increasing number of good people around to choose from. Those who do secure sponsorship would normally expect to serve their articles with that firm. Occasionally a longer commitment to employment is demanded.

Clifford Chance, a leading international law firm, recruits 130 trainee lawyers each year. All trainees recruited can apply for a scholarship awarded to assist with the costs of the Law Society's professional exams. The scholarship will cover the cost of tuition fees and a contribution towards the trainees' living costs.

**2. Summer Vacation Placement Programmes.** A number of firms run Vacation Placement Programmes for second-year undergraduates when they will size you up for a training contract. To get accepted for a course is in itself an achievement, but it is certainly no guarantee of success.

**3. Law Society Bursary Scheme.** Available for students taking CPE and LPC, it is very limited, competitive and includes hardship criteria – but worth trying. The bursary is made up from a variety of funds and grant-making trusts which have been grouped together under an umbrella scheme. Applications from the beginning of March.
Contact: Legal Information Services, The Law Society, Ipsley Court, Berrington Close, Redditch, Worcestershire B98 0TD. Tel: 01527 504 433.

**4. Local authority grants.** Local authorities are not obliged to fund CPE or LPC students, and rarely do. But they do have discretionary funds available for a wide range of courses and, providing you meet their criteria for awards, you could strike lucky. There are no hard and fast rules, as every local authority has its own. Your local authority may well issue a leaflet giving information on study areas eligible for financial support. Enquire at your local education authority. Failing that contact the Law Society.

**5. Ethnic Minority Law Bursaries Scheme.** A limited number of bursaries are available for the Legal Practice Course and Bar Vocational Course, for ethnic minority students who are British Citizens and want to qualify as solicitors. Bursaries are worth £4000 and include four weeks' work experience. The scheme is backed by a number of legal firms and companies and operated by the Windsor Fellowship who can be contacted for more details at 47, Hackney Road, London E2 7NX. Tel: 0171 613 0373.

**6. Loans** If all other lines of attack have failed there is always a LOAN (see page 174).

*Warning note:* If you haven't already got Articles, getting through law school isn't necessarily a passport to a position in a law firm.

# What about other professional qualifications?

Accountants, engineers, actuaries – usually join firms who specialise in that kind of work. The firm will pay for your training and pay you while you are being trained.

# OK, so nobody is going to fund me – can I get a loan?

Yes. There are four excellent schemes.

## 1. THE CAREER DEVELOPMENT LOAN

Available only to those taking a vocational training of up to two years. You can borrow up to £8000 and not less than £300. The loan is designed to cover course fees (only 80% given if you are in full employment) plus books, materials and living expenses where applicable. The loan is provided by the banks (Barclays, Co-operative, Clydesdale, The Royal Bank of Scotland). Interest on the loan is paid by the government while you are studying and for one month after your course has finished (or up to six months if you are unemployed when repayment should start). If your course costs more than you can borrow your local Training and Enterprise Council (TEC) may sponsor you for the additional amount. Check them out. Phone 0800 585 505 for free booklet on Career Development Loans.

## 2. THE BUSINESS SCHOOL LOAN SCHEME

If you are wanting to take an MBA then the Association of MBAs (AMBA) should be able to help. It runs a special scheme to assist graduates and other suitable applicants to study for a Master's degree in Business Administration. The scheme is run in conjunction with Barclays and NatWest banks. To take advantage of the scheme you need to have a bachelor's degree or other suitable professional qualification, a minimum of two years' relevant work experience or five years' experience in industry or commerce, and to have secured yourself a place on an MBA course at a business school which is on the Association's approved list. Maximum loan for full-time students is two-thirds of present or last gross salary plus tuition fees for each year of study. Preferential interest rates are given during the course. Repayment starts three months after completion of your course and you have up to seven years to pay it off.

### 3. LAW SCHOOL LOANS

Assisted by the Law Society, two major banks (NatWest and Barclays) run a special scheme to help students fund CPE and Legal Practice Courses. The loan, which currently stands at up to £15,000 is given at very favourable rates. For more details and an application form contact either NatWest or Barclays direct.

### 4. POSTGRADUATE LOAN – see chart page 176.

## I want to study abroad – can I get help?

Raising finance for postgraduate study abroad is even more difficult, though not completely impossible. Competition is fierce and the opportunities small. The most likely sources are the very limited number of scholarships given to foreign students by the government of host countries or individual institutions. *The European Choice* published by the DfEE is a good starting point for those interested in studying in Europe. *Study Abroad* published by UNESCO is the best reference source for international scholarships. Otherwise contact the British Council or specific embassies.

Many countries produce special literature for foreign students which they will send you. The Commonwealth Scholarship and Fellowship plan is a possible source for those from one commonwealth country visiting another commonwealth country. If you are thinking of the USA then the Fulbright Commission is the best place to start as it administers the annual competition for the Fulbright awards. Leaflets from the Commission covering all aspects of postgraduate study in the USA are available, including details on tuition fees and awards.

Check out: SOCRATES-ERASMUS and LEONARDO, page 52

---

## Cash crisis note

If you have just graduated and already have a loan to pay off, think twice before getting even further into debt.

---

## What help is there for students coming to the UK from abroad?

There are scholarships specifically for overseas students, but these are few, so apply early. The Overseas Research Students Award Scheme

# What loans do banks offer to postgraduates?

**Bank of Scotland:**

Professional Study Loan

Up to £6000 for one year
£8000 for two years

**Barclays:**

Business School Loan

Full-time students: Two-thirds of previous salary plus course fees. Part-time students: Amount of course fees and related expenses. £10,000 max

Professional Study Loan (Medicine, Dentistry, Optometry, Veterinary Science)

£20,000 max for Law Students

Career Development Loan (for vocational training lasting at least one week)

£300 min; £8000 max

**Clydesdale:**

Postgraduate Loan (courses at Strathclyde, Stirling & Dundee Universities)

Two-thirds previous salary or £2000pa, plus course fees

Career Development Loan (for vocational training lasting at least one week)

£300 min; £8000 max

Professional Studies Loan

Up to £6000

**Co-operative:**

Career Development Loan

£300 min; £8000 max

**Lloyds:**

£500 to £5,000 for 6 months (min) to 60 months (max). Graduates have the option of no repayments for the first 4 months. Graduate Loan Repayment Protection Insurance.

**Midland:**

Professional Studies Loan: Medical/ Dental/Veterinary

£10,000 plus course fees over 2 years

Legal and other

£10,000 plus course fees over 2 years
£5000 plus course fees over 1 year

**NatWest:**

Professional Trainee Loan: Trainee Barrister Trainee Solicitor Other professions ie Doctor, Dentist, Pharmacist, Vet etc MBA

£15,000 – ten years to repay loan

**Royal Bank of Scotland:**

Medical Loan for clinical years

up to £10,000

Law School Loan

up to £10,000

Career Development Loan

up to £8000
£1000 to £5000 for recent graduates.

**TSB:**

Preferential overdraft facility for graduates one year after completion of studies.
Graduates can also apply for a non-secured personal loan.

provides awards annually on a competitive basis to overseas postgraduate students of outstanding merit and research potential. (Between 750 and 800 awards are likely to be given during the academic year 1998–99.) The awards are tenable at any of 190 academic institutions in the UK. Each award will cover the difference between the tuition fee for a home (UK) postgraduate student and the fee charged to overseas postgraduate students. The award can be made for any field of study.

The only criteria for the awards are outstanding merit and research potential; other factors such as means, nationality, proposed field and institution of study, will not be taken into account. The scheme is run by the committee of Vice-Chancellors and Principals of the Universities of the UK and a special committee of senior academic staff select award holders. For further details and application form contact the Registrar or Secretary at the academic institution where you want to study. Closing day for applications is usually towards the end of April. Or phone Caroline Seal, ORS Administrator on 0171 419 5498/9.

The best source for finance is your own home government. Failing that, try the British Government through the British Council, the Foreign and Commonwealth Office or the Overseas Development Agency schemes. There are also the Commonwealth Scholarship Plan, the UN and other international organisations. Some universities give awards and scholarships specially to students from abroad – but each university needs to be contacted individually. Some charitable trusts also cater for foreign students. EGAS (see details on page 149) should be able to help you winkle them out, or check for yourself in appropriate directories (see bibliography on next page). EU students can compete for UK postgraduate awards already listed in this chapter, but on a fees basis only.

## As a student from abroad, what is it really going to cost?

**Fees** – There is no set rate of fees for postgraduate courses. In the past there has been a recommended minimum but each institution can charge what it wants. Fees for overseas students are generally substantially more than those for home students. EU nationals are generally eligible for home UK student rates. Science courses are usually more expensive than those for the arts.

*Average overseas postgraduate fees in 1997/98 were:*

| | |
|---|---|
| Arts: | £6300 |
| Science: | £8200 |
| Clinical: | £15,400 |

**Living expenses** – Our survey in Chapter 1 will give you some idea of what things in Britain are likely to cost. But students with no family close at hand for support are likely to find their needs are more. As a rule of thumb, students from abroad will need at least £8000–£9000pa if studying in London or Oxford and Cambridge, and not less than £6000–£8000pa if studying elsewhere.  In addition, in the first year you could need up to £500 for books and equipment; another £400–£500 for warm clothing if you come from a hot climate. A deposit on rented accommodation could set you back a further £250–£400 and temporary accommodation while you are seeking somewhere to live could cost £30–£50 a night.

## Who to contact/What to read

- *Awards for Postgraduate Study at Commonwealth Universities*, ACU biennial.
- *Awards to Women for Graduate Research 1994/95*, British Federation of University Women Graduates, South Bank Business Centre, Park House, 140 Battersea Park Road, London SW11 4NB.
- *British Universities Guide to Graduate Study*, Association of Commonwealth Universities.
- *The Directory of Graduate Studies*, complete guide to 6000 postgraduate courses in the UK. CRAC, Hobsons Publishing.
- *How to Choose Your MBA* and *How to Choose Your Postgraduate Course*, Trotman.
- *POSTGRAD* series covering Engineering, Science, and Information Technology, published by Hobsons, or free from your university.
- *Postgraduate Management Education*, Graduate Careers Information Booklet – AGCAS The Association of Graduate Careers Advisory Services (as above). *Free from your Careers Service.*
- *Postgraduate Study*, Hobsons.
- *Postgraduate Study and Research*, Graduate Careers Information Booklet updated regularly – AGCAS The Association of Graduate Careers Advisory Services, CSU (Publications) Ltd, Armstrong House, Oxford Road, Manchester M1 7ED. Tel: 0161 277 5200. *Free from your Careers Service.*

- *PROSPECTS POSTGRAD*, options for further study and research. CSU (Publications) Ltd. Issued once a term.

**For law students**

- *Prospects Legal* which incorporates *ROSET* (Register of Solicitors Employing Trainees), the most comprehensive information about firms offering sponsorship, available from university or careers services or by direct mail from CSU Ltd, Armstrong House, Oxford Road, Manchester M17 ED. Tel: 0161 237 5409.
- *The Lawyer Magazine 'Student Special'*, a supplement published twice a year generally around May and September, which lists firms willing to sponsor students. It also organises a fair in London in November each year, when students can meet representatives of law firms and it will pay a subsidy towards the fares of students wishing to attend. *The Lawyer*, 50 Poland Street, London W1V 4AX. Tel: 0171 439 4222; also: www.the-Lawyer.co.uk.
- *PROSPECTS Legal VacWork*, available from your own careers service or CSU Ltd.

**For study abroad**

- *Awards for Postgraduate Study at Commonwealth Universities* and *Commonwealth Universities Year-Book*, Association of Commonwealth Universities.
- *Study Abroad, International Scholarships, International Courses* – UNESCO, HMSO, PO Box 276, London SW8 5DT.
- *Guide to Awards Open to British Graduate Students For Study in Canada*, Canada House, Trafalgar Square, London SW1Y 5BJ.
- *Assistance for Students in Australia and the UK*, Australian High Commission, Australia House, London WC2B 4LA.
- *Scholarships and Funding for Study and Research in Germany*, German Academic Exchange Service, 17 Bloomsbury Square, London WC1A 2LP.
- *Postgraduate Information Pack*, on applying, tuition fees etc. Educational Advisory Service, The Fulbright Commission, Fulbright House, 62 Doughty Street, London WC1N 2LS.

**For foreign students studying in the UK**

- *British University and College Courses*, Trotman.
- *Sources of Funding for International Students*, free from the British Council, Bridgewater House, 58 Whitworth Street, Manchester M16 BB. Tel: 0161 957 7755.

- *Studying and Living in Britain*, annual handbook, a British Council publication available from Northcote House Publisher, Plymbridge House, Estover Road, Plymouth, PL6 7PY. Tel: 01752 202 301.
- *The International Students A–Z: A Guide to Studying and Living in London.* Published annually by International Students House, The British Council London Conference on Overseas Students, available from the British Council, Bridgewater House, 58 Whitworth Street, Manchester M16 BB.

# 7
# MAKING THE MONEY GO ROUND

## Advice on budgeting

In this final chapter, we try to give you some advice on how to manage your money with the help of students, Leeds University Welfare Service and a bank manager who has first-hand knowledge of some of the financial difficulties students get themselves into, and how best to help them.

## Problems and Predicaments

*'My rent is over £55 a week. There's gas and electricity and telephone on top of that, I'm not making ends meet.'*

*'I've got an overdraft of £900, the bank is charging interest; if I've got an overdraft how can I pay the interest charges?'*

*"I thought: £1000, wow!" at the beginning of the term and blew the lot in the -rst few weeks. I haven't even the money for my train fare home.'*

*'I'm a geography student and have to go on a compulsory trip. Where on earth am I going to find £80?'*

*'I know now that I shouldn't have bought the car and spent all that money on booze, but ...'*

*'Debt – it just crept up on me without my really noticing.'*

## A bank manager's view

Over £4,000 from your grant and student loan! – It certainly sounds a lot, but is it really? If all you are receiving is the standard funding for students then you haven't got wealth beyond your dreams, but the absolute minimum for survival. Bear that in mind, right from the start and every time temptation looms, then you shouldn't go far wrong. There will always be those who like to live on the edge, spend now and cope with debt and disaster later. Most students who get into debt are genuinely surprised at how easily the money "just slipped through" their bank account. As the student said, it has a way of just creeping up on you if you let it. So be warned.

# WHAT IS BUDGETING?

The principles are incredibly simple. Putting them into practice is, for many people, incredibly hard. It is a matter of working out what your income and expenses are and making sure the latter doesn't exceed the former. It may sound rather boring, but it's a lot better than being in debt. The students quoted on the previous page obviously didn't budget.

## Where to keep your money – bank, building society, under the mattress?

Before you can start budgeting you need to choose somewhere to keep your money. We would recommend either a bank or a building society. They are generally quite keen to attract students' accounts because they see students as potential high earners. Earlier in this book there are details of the different freebies the banks offer to entice students to join them. These are worth studying, but shouldn't be the deciding factor. More important is to choose a bank or building society which is located close to your home or place of study. While these days you can use the cash dispensing machines in most branches of most banks and building societies, they haven't yet invented a machine that can give advice.

# WHAT TYPE OF ACCOUNT?

There are a number of different types of account. At the bank you'll need to open what's called a current account so you can draw money out at any time. Many banks offer accounts specially designed for students, so it's worth checking with them. Some current accounts give interest. It is not as much as a savings account, but every little helps. Check your bank for interest rates.

A building society current account is very similar to a bank account. They too give instant access to your money, and also pay interest on any money in your account. How much depends on the going rate and your building society.

## Shop around

If you are looking for a bank account Leeds University advises students to shop around and compare the banks and what they can offer you in terms of overdrafts etc. If you want an overdraft, the simplest way to compare charges is to ask for the EAR 'Effective Annual Rate'. This is a standardised way of expressing the total cost of borrowing if you were continually overdrawn for a year. It is, they advise, also worthwhile asking the following questions:

- How much interest will I earn if I am in credit?
- Do I get a free overdraft facility? If so, how much?
- If I want to arrange a larger overdraft will I be charged an arrangement fee?
- What will the interest rate be on my overdraft?
- If I am overdrawn without consent how much will I be charged for:
- the unauthorised balance
- the bounced cheques?

## What will you get when you open an account?

When you open an account you may receive a:

- **Cheque book** which you can use to pay big bills and for large purchases.
- **Cheque guarantee card** which could be up to £100. This states that the bank will guarantee your cheque up to the amount shown on the card and so the shop where you are making your purchase will let you take the goods away there and then.

- **Cash card** which enables you to withdraw cash from a cash machine, and may offer additional payment functions.

- **PIN number** – this is your own Personal Identification Number which you will need to remember and use when getting money from the cash dispenser.

- **Debit card (SOLO, Switch or Delta)** which will automatically debit your account for goods bought when passed through a terminal at the point of sale.

- **The three-in-one card** Most banks and building societies combine the facilities mentioned above into multifunctional cards which act as cheque guarantee cards, give access to cash machines and can be used as debit cards so you can purchase goods and services without writing a cheque.

- **Account number** which you will need for any correspondence with your bank.

- **Paying-in book** containing paying-in slips, probably with your branch name printed on them, which you can use when paying in cheques and money. Just fill in the slip and pass it to your bank. Most banks provide pre-printed envelopes which you can pick up in your branch and then post through a letter box in the banking hall.

- **Statement** sent to you at regular intervals (we would advise you to ask for it monthly). The statement will give details of the money going in and out of your account – an essential part of budgeting properly.

---

## Caution

Don't keep your cheque guarantee card and cheque book together. If stolen, somebody could clean out your account.

Keep your Personal Identification Number (PIN) secret. Never write it down or tell it to anyone else.

Cheques take three days to clear from an account. So don't go on a mad spending spree if you find you have more money in your account than you thought. The read-out on the cash machine may not be up to date.

## Your income – how much?

It's all very well to have an official piggy bank in which to keep your money, but where is the money going to come from and how much is it likely to be? If you have read the rest of this book, you should by now have some idea how much you are likely to have as a student. If you look at our budgeting plan, we have listed some of the likely sources. With a little ingenuity you may have discovered others.

Now let's get down to it.

## Work out a simple budgeting plan

1. Take a piece of paper and divide into three columns. One the left-hand side write down your likely income sources and how much they will provide, for example:

   ● grant
   ● parental contribution
   ● student loan
   ● money from access fund
   ● money earned from holiday job
   ● sponsorship etc.

   Now total them up.

   The trouble with budgeting, especially for students, is that money generally comes in at one time, often in large chunks at the beginning of a term, and your outgoings at another. When you work you will probably find it easiest to budget on a monthly basis, but as a student you will probably have to do it either termly or yearly depending on how the money comes in.

2. In the middle column write down your fixed expenses – things that you have to pay out like rent, gas, electricity, telephone, food etc. Don't forget to include fares. Now total them up.

3. Subtract your fixed expenses from your income and you will see just how much you have, or haven't, got left over to spend.

   Draw a line under the list in your right hand column and now list your incidental expenses, things like socialising, clothes, the cinema, hobbies, birthdays, etc. This is your 'do without column': the area where you can juggle your expenses to make ends meet.

| INCOME | | OUTGOINGS | | |
| --- | --- | --- | --- | --- |
| | | *Predicted* | | *Actual* |
| Grant | £ | Rent/College Board | £ | £ |
| Parental Contrib. | £ | Gas | £ | £ |
| Student Loan | £ | Electricity | £ | £ |
| Sponsorship | £ | Telephone | £ | £ |
| Holiday Job | £ | Launderette/cleaning | £ | £ |
| Access Fund | £ | Food | £ | £ |
| | | Fares while in college | £ | £ |
| | | Fares to college | £ | £ |
| | | Car expenses | £ | £ |
| | | Books/Equipment | £ | £ |
| | | Compulsory trips | £ | £ |
| | | TV licence | £ | £ |
| | | Student rail/bus card | £ | £ |
| **Total:** | £ | **Total:** | £ | |
| | | .................................... | | .............. |
| | | Socialising | £ | £ |
| | | Hobbies | £ | £ |
| | | Entertainment | £ | £ |
| | | Clothes | £ | £ |
| | | Presents | £ | £ |
| | | Holidays | £ | £ |

4. Apportion what's left over to the things listed in this final column making sure you've got at least something left over for emergencies. Do the figures add up?

Seems simple enough and logical on paper. But of course it doesn't work quite as easily as that. There's always the unexpected. You can't get a job. Your car needs a new battery. People use more gas than expected. Did you really talk for that long on the phone?

5. Having worked out your budget, use the final column on your budget sheet to fill in exactly how much your bills do come to. In this way you can keep a check on your outgoings and how accurate your predictions were, and do something BEFORE the money runs out.

## What is a standing order?

Regular payments such as rent can be paid automatically by the bank through a standing order. You just tell the bank how much to pay out

---

## Thrift tips

*'Try to live near college and far away from a pub,'* 4th year Business Studies student, Portsmouth

*'Access funds aren't widely advertised. I got £200 to repay money I had borrowed from a friend,'* 3rd year Sociology student, Aberdeen

*'Try to get your booklist early then you are first in line for second-hand books,'* 4th year Dentistry student, Dundee

*'House kitties save loads – eat and cook together,'* 4th year Engineering student, Bristol

*'Take a gap year and save,'* 4th year Biochemistry student, Surrey

---

and to whom and they will do the rest. The system is ideal for people who are bad at getting round to paying their bills. Forget to pay the electricity and you'll soon know. Standing orders are not so easy to organise when you are in shared accommodation with everyone chipping in on the bill.

## What is a direct debit?

With a direct debit again the bill is paid automatically, but it works in a different way. The bank of the organisation you are paying the money to will collect the money direct from your account. This is an ideal way of paying when the amount being paid out is likely to change.

## Cards and the catches

**Credit cards:** These are an easy way to pay for things but can also be an easy way to get into debt. When you have a card such as Mastercard, Visa or Barclaycard, you are given a credit limit. This means you can make purchases up to that sum. Each month you receive a statement of how much you owe. If you pay back the whole lot immediately there are no interest charges. If you don't, you will pay interest on the balance. There is an annual charge for credit cards. You can use your card in the UK and abroad at most shops and many restaurants. They are a way of getting short-term credit but are an expensive way of borrowing long term. On the plus side they are a way to spread payments or ease temporary cashflow problems.

**Store cards:** Many stores, such as Marks & Spencer, offer credit cards which operate in much the same way as described above, but can only be used in that particular store or chain of stores. Although most stores will check your credit rating before issuing you with a card, they are still too easy to come by – get a stack of them and you could find you're 'seriously' in debt.

**Debit cards:** You've probably seen the Switch card in action as many stores and garages now have the Switch system installed: look for the green Switch logo. By simply passing your debit card through a Switch terminal, the price of the purchase you are making is automatically deducted from your account. What could be easier? Details of the transaction will show up on your next statement.

**SAFETY CHECK:** most banks and building societies will NOT send plastic cards or pin numbers to customers living in halls of residence or multi-occupancy lodging, because they could go astray or sit in the hall way for days unclaimed. All too easy to steal. You may have to collect them from a branch nearby.

---

## Caution
Don't borrow from a lot of places. If you've got an overdraft and a Student Loan, that's probably enough.

---

# WHAT IF THE MONEY RUNS OUT?

## Help, I am in debt!

Don't panic, but don't sweep the matter under the carpet and try to ignore it because it won't go away. In fact it will just get worse. Get in touch with your Student Welfare Officer at your university, or the student adviser at your local university branch, or your bank manager. Or all three. Through experience they will be able to give the best advice and help. Impoverished and imprudent students are not a new phenomenon.

# Getting an overdraft

You don't get 'owt' for 'nowt' – well rarely. Most banks are fairly generous to students and do allow them to be overdrawn sometimes without charging. If you look back in this book at the section on 'What the Banks Offer' (pages 78-9), you'll see they do offer free overdraft facilities to students up to around £750 in their first year of study, however this can increase in subsequent years of study. BUT DON'T TAKE IT AS A RIGHT. Always ask your bank first if it will grant you this facility. Otherwise you will be in trouble and could be charged. And remember whatever you borrow eventually has to be paid back.

If you find yourself overdrawn, get on the phone or call in immediately to your bank. Many of the clearing banks have campus branches or at least a branch in the town geared to dealing with students. They'll probably be sympathetic and come up with a helpful solution.

# Borrowing on credit

*'Haven't got the money at the moment so I'll buy it on Mastercard.'*

Easily done, but be warned, though Mastercard/Visa is excellent as a payment card, credit can cause problems. If you don't pay off your bill by the date given on your statement, you will have to pay interest and, compared with other sources of borrowing, this is very high. Unlike your friendly bank, credit card companies are not the sort of people you can negotiate with, and are very likely to sue. Don't see them as another source of income.

# A planned overdraft

*'I'm going for an interview and need something to wear.'*

This is not an unusual request from students in their final year. Banks are very good at coming up with a plan to help you out with an obvious or specific need. After all, an interview success could mean you'll clear your overdraft that much quicker.

An overdraft is often the cheapest way of borrowing, but there are charges and interest rates, which need to be checked out. The advantage of an overdraft is that you don't have to pay it back in fixed amounts, though the bank has the right to ask for its money back at any time.

## Personal loans

This is quite different from an overdraft. It is usually used when you want to borrow a much larger sum, over a longer period – say several years. It differs from an overdraft in that you borrow an agreed amount over a set period of time and the repayments are a fixed amount, generally monthly. You might take out a loan to pay for your course fees but not for short-term credit to tide you over until your next grant cheque arrives.

## How the student adviser can help

Don't be afraid to go into your bank and ask for help. Most banks have specially trained student advisers on the premises, to help students like you. They will arrange bank accounts, discuss overdrafts, help with budgeting. It's what they've been trained for. Many of them have recently been students, so they know the ropes – and the difficulties.

## Don'ts

**(Which unfortunately some students do)**

- Don't fall into the hands of a loan shark. Any loan offered to students, except from a recognised student source, ie the banks, building societies, parents or the Student Loan Scheme, should be treated

---

### Thrift tips

Leeds University Union Welfare Services suggests these ways for managing your money:

- Get value for money – use markets, or large supermarkets for fresh fruit and vegetables – your local corner shop may be convenient, but is often more expensive.
- Make the most of student discounts for coach and rail travel, clubs, restaurants and hairdresser.
- Use the library rather than buying books – has your Uni got a second-hand bookshop?
- Withdraw only the amount of cash you actually need on a weekly basis from the bank – otherwise it will disappear.

with the utmost caution and suspicion. It's bound to cost you an arm and a leg, and lead to trouble.

- Don't run up an overdraft with your bank without asking first – even the much vaunted interest free overdraft offered by most banks to students should be checked out first, otherwise you might find you are being charged. They need to know you are a student.

- Don't forget to pay your gas and electricity bills. Make them top priority. A week or two on bread and (cheap) jam is better than having to pay court costs.

- Don't pawn your guitar, only to find you can't afford to get it out to play at the next gig.

- Don't try 'kiting'. The banks have got wind of what's been going on, and you're bound to be found out and in real trouble. For the uninitiated like this author, kiting is the dishonest practice of making the most of the time lapse between people reporting that their credit card is missing, and it being recorded as stolen. Be warned, it is a criminal offence, and could end up increasing your debts – or even worse.

- Don't get black-listed with the bank. 'Kiting' is a sure way of getting a bad record. Running up an overdraft is another.

- Don't see credit cards as another source of income.

## Savings?

Most books on budgeting give lengthy advice on saving. We think it unlikely that students will do more than just make ends meet, and even that will be a struggle. However, if you do find that you have some surplus cash, or have taken out the Student Loan as an investment, it would be advisable to open a savings account at a bank, a building society or the Post Office. Check out the interest rates and the terms and

---

### A bank manager's view

The problems students have are very real. As a bank manager, all too often we find we are just picking up the pieces when things have gone too far. Debt brings stress, and that will affect your ability to study. Come sooner rather than later.

conditions. Many high-interest accounts give limited access to your money – so, watch out.

We thought we'd let a student have the final word:

*'Before they start a degree students don't realise just how tough it's going to be. You think, how on earth can anybody be so irresponsible as to get £12,000 worth of debt? But once you are into university life, you know only too well. Despite the hardship, don't be put off, university is excellent – an incredible experience not to be missed!'*

**Best of luck ...**

# 5% OFF YOUR CAREERS ANNUALS FOR EVER!

Selected annual Careers titles are available from Trotman on Standing Order. Enter your Standing Order for any of these titles NOW, and we will invoice you each year at 5% OFF the published price!

YES PLEASE! Enter my Standing Order for the following titles:

| ✔ | Qty | Title |
|---|-----|-------|
| ❏ | ....... | **The Student Book** |
| ❏ | ....... | **Degree Course Offers** |
| ❏ | ....... | **How To Complete Your UCAS Form** |
| ❏ | ....... | **Art & Design Courses (On Course)** |
| ❏ | ....... | **\*The Big Official UCAS Guide To University & College Entrance** |
| ❏ | ....... | **\*The NATFHE Handbook of Initial Teacher Training** |
| ❏ | ....... | **\*Occupations** |

\*Please ensure there is no existing standing order arrangement with the publisher.

I understand that Trotman & Co. will send me the above titles each year at a 5% discount (starting with the editions due for publication in 1998), and that a new invoice will be issued with each delivery.

Signed: ...............................................................................

Date:...................................................................................

Name: .................................................................................

Organisation: .....................................................................

Address: .............................................................................

...............................................................................................

...............................................................................................

## Please complete this sheet, and fax it to us on:
# 0181 332 7253